HOME
in the Twenties and Thirties

This and the tailpiece are from woodcuts by Eric Revilious 1936.

HOME
in the Twenties and Thirties

Mary and Neville Ward

LONDON
IAN ALLAN LTD

CONTENTS

First published 1978

ISBN 0 7110 0785 3 (Casebound edition)
ISBN 0 7110 0904 x (Paperback edition)

Design by Ian Crawford, DA(Edin), LSIAD

© Neville Ward 1978

Published by Ian Allan Ltd, Shepperton, Surrey,
and printed in the United Kingdom by
Ian Allan Printing Ltd.

FOREWORD

This collection of pictures started from a discussion with some contemporaries about our childhood. We were comparing attitudes to the clothes we wore and the homes we occupied. We were all the beneficiaries of secure and happy homes, firm and loving parents.

Earliest memories related to a slim Mum in a short dress, whereas recall of the same lady ten years later suggested that for an evening occasion Mum was a well-rounded lady in a backless gown which reached to the floor. Homes did not reveal the same consistency as did one lady and another, nor the same marked change of fashion over a decade. Home stayed the same, apart from minor changes like the first wireless set or a new set of curtains. One, or even two, cataclysmic changes perhaps when home moved from one house to another – in those cases (rather like Mum) though the form changed the content remained fundamentally the same.

The disparity of attitude to clothes and homes, we all agreed in our talk, was a matter of economics. Buying a house was the task of a lifetime; furnishings were bought to last. Comfort was a prime consideration; only the lunatic fringe would countenance a chair which demanded bodily discipline or distortion in use. Clothes, we thought, did not respond to the same criteria.

Such discussions are a commonplace after an evening meal and are generally forgotten the next day. This one,

this time, sparked off an urge to check our memories against the facts. We read books and collected pictures, visited scenes we knew and some we had only heard about. Memory was sound but not very well informed. We were shamed by constant evidence of hardship and deprivation but we enjoyed reading that in 1933 the Army and Navy Stores could supply a packet of ant eggs for twopence and a baby grand piano for 85 guineas. We were intrigued to visit Bournville and find the word meant more than a tuppeny bar of chocolate. The weights and measures to which we refer may be perplexing: 1 pound weight (lb) is 0.454 of a kilogram; 1 yard length is 0.914 of a metre; 12 old pence made 1 shilling; 20 shillings 1 pound sterling; 21 shillings a guinea; 5d is five old pence, 2s 6d is two shillings and six pence.

The acknowledgements on page 128 are a list of people and organisations who were unfailingly kind helpful and generous to us. As a result we found ourselves with many pictures some of which are the content of this book. They are here as an amusement, and no more than that, whether, like us, you recall the twenties and thirties or think them a remote and peculiar past. A great deal is missing; there is no social message or academic endeavour. It is a sort of salad of our salad days; days which in George Orwell's words seemed for some of us to be . . . Summer all the year round.

The inter-war years were by no means a summer all the time. Helpless poverty contrasted with often unfeeling affluence. In almost every aspect of life, from the transitory determinations of politicians to the eternal preoccupations of artists, there was controversy. Communism or Fascism, Constructivism or Realism and on down the line to long hair or short, gas cooking or electric. Large decisions which most individuals found it difficult to understand let alone comment upon or influence, small decisions which seemed more and more subject to the outside influences of commercial persuasion.

It's not surprising that home was important; that between those two wartime periods when brutality and compassion were somehow fused into an apparently coherent philosophy the family concern was comfort, security and a certain defiant statement of individuality. Not surprising that those concerns seemed most tangibly satisfied and expressed in and by the Home.

Home was one room housing an entire family, was a large mansion in which there were as many servants as served. Between these extremes were every sort and condition.

For the majority it was living room, parlour, kitchen, two bedrooms, one box room, bath and a small garden. For many that home would be located not in the town, nor the country, but in a twilight zone which was massively developed, called Suburbia.

Housing developments on the outskirts of a town or city were no novelty in the twenties. The scale of the work, encouraged by improved transport facilities and some adjustment to the class and financial structure of society, make suburban development the dominant characteristic of inter-war home building. About four million houses were constructed in the twenties and thirties, most of them contributing to the creation of new suburbs.

The mood of the suburbs seems in retrospect tranquil. Many an occupier felt he shared in the pleasures of both town and country. The best of both worlds. The best of all worlds. Really the summers *were* extraordinarily long. Sitting in a deck chair in the garden one could just catch the smell of the pinks in the border. Traffic noises limited to neighbours lawn mower or the bakers delivery van.

The house was fresh and polished, the clink of tea cups, the slumbering dog lifting one eye and twitching an ear at the prospect of a biscuit when the family gathered round the afternoon tray. And even when summer merged into winter it was cosy. Long leisurely nights with the cold dismissed by a flickering coal fire, the children allowed as a special treat to put on the electric radiator and play with the train set in the front room, Arthur Askey in *Bandwaggon* on the wireless and a glass of warm milk to guarantee a good nights sleep before Father's catching the 8.15 in the morning.

The aesthetic of the suburbs was less sure than the mood. Indeed it was the despair of not only architects but also of those people who cared for the traditions of town or country life.

Town and country did have strong traditions in the making of homes, no less than in other activities related to place. For some, tradition was confused with preservation and the period was one in which a reluctance to accept change allowed a continuance of watery and miniscule impersonation of past styles of building. Others took the more vigorous attitude of positively rejecting traditions or of looking for an extension of past traditions to meet the challenge of new circumstances.

T. S. Eliot, in 1934, made articulate what we may believe were the feelings of many people when he wrote 'We are always in danger, in clinging to an old tradition, or attempting to re-establish one, of confusing the vital and the unessential, the real and the sentimental . . . what we can do is use our minds, remembering that a tradition without intelligence is not worth having, to discover what is the best life for us not as political abstraction, but as a particular people in a particular place.'

In town and country, then, the inter-war years saw the building of homes as near reproduction antiques as mass production methods and modern convenience would allow, all contrasted with homes stripped of mouldings or any purely decorative embellishment, uncompromisingly cubic in form and exhibiting large expanses of glass set into white rendered walls.

But for the new suburbs no tradition was formed to either embrace or reject. There was no vital inheritance and the builder fell back on a free adaption of the non-essentials of the past used in a bewildering juxtaposition not only between one pair of houses (for that was how they were generally built) and another but in the form and on the facades of individual structures. It may have been stylistic indigestion but it became the vernacular architecture and its admirers were, quite properly, its users.

It is unlikely that, at any time or in any place, there had ever before been such diversity in form and decoration of houses – and the contents which transformed these houses into homes revealed an equally ambivalent attitude to furnishings. While some familes struggled to maintain a consistency of style (at least within each room if not throughout the building) others enjoyed a touch of modernity in the wireless on the Jacobean style sideboard – or the softening influence of simulated candles, parchment shaded, at either side of the latest 'modernist' bed.

Never mind. Ancient or Modern; Plain or Fancy; Luxurious or Austere; home is an affair of the heart.

1920

In this position, under the heading for every third year from 1921 to 1939, is a short shopping list of items in common use with prices from the current lists of the Army and Navy Stores in London. Except for 1921, which was expensive, prices were remarkably stable. From 1924 to 1939 the price of soap, beer, and cigarettes stayed the same. Only a few items varied greatly, such as cameras; the most expensive in 1921 was £22 and in 1939 was £78 5s, but that was surely to do with the increased complexity of the equipment. More mysteriously, a ten-pound wedding cake fell in price consistently from £2 2s 6d in 1921 to £1 5s in 1939.

In January the Allied and Associated Powers appeared to have established a peace settlement embodying the five treaties which ended the First World War. The League of Nations was established and survivors hoped, no doubt, for better things in the 1920s.

The King had said in 1919 that 'an adequate solution of the housing question is the foundation of all social progress'.

Lord Long was more explicit: 'It would be a black crime, indeed, if we were to sit still and do nothing by way of preparation to ensure that when these men come back they should be provided with homes with as little delay as possible. To let them come back from the horrible waterlogged trenches to something little better than a pig-sty here would indeed be criminal on the part of ourselves, and would be a negation of all that has been said during the war'.

The lower picture, taken in 1920, is of a family living in a pig shed in Woking. They would probably have envied the demobbed soldier living in a canvas hut at Ongar, but neither could be expected to think they had been rewarded by a suitable hero's home. They probably shared Lord Long's view that they were suffering a black crime. As for the unhappy couple in the Punch cartoon, we can readily believe they had turned from many an estate agent's door on reading a note similar to those recalled in Arnold Bennett's Journal for March, to the effect that there were no unfurnished houses or flats to let under £160 per annum.

The Government were in some despair. In the twelve months up to the end of March only 715 new houses had been completed in England and Wales compared with an estimated need of something like six hundred thousand.

The Incomparable Max erred a little in timing with his light-hearted essay on 'Homes Unblest'.

'. . . . I beheld, this morning, on a road near the coast of Norfolk, a railway-car without wheels. Without wheels though it was, it had motion – of a kind; of a kind worse than actual stagnation. Mounted on a very long steam-lorry that groaned and panted, it very slowly passed me.

. . . . I decided that I would slowly follow.

. . . . The tracks led me at last through a lane and thence into sight of a little bay, on whose waters were perceptible the sleek heads of sundry human beings, and on its sands the full-lengths of sundry other human beings in bath-robes, reading novels or merely basking.

. . . . This land was dominated by a crescent of queer little garish tenements, the like of which I had never seen, nor would wish to see again. They did not stand on the ground, but on stakes of wood and shafts of brick, six feet or so above the ground's level, and were led up to by flights of wooden steps that tried not to look like ladders. They displeased me much. They had little railed platforms round them, and things hanging out to dry on the railings; and their walls vied unneighbourly with one another in lawless colour-schemes. One tenement was salmon-pink with wide bands of scarlet, another sky-blue with a key-pattern in orange, and so on around the whole little horrid array. And I deduced, from certain upstanding stakes and shafts at the nearer end of the crescent, that the horror was not complete yet.

. . . . I had once heard that disused railway-cars were convertible into seaside cottages. But the news had not fired my imagination not protruded in my memory. Today, as an eye-witness of the accomplished fact, I was impressed, sharply enough, and I went nearer to the crescent, drawn by a sort of dreadful fascination. I found that the cottages all had names. One cottage was Mermaid's Rock; another (which had fluttering window curtains of Stuart tartan), Spray o' the Sea; another, The Nest; another, Brinynook; and yet another had been named, with less fitness, but in an ampler and to me more interesting spirit, Petworth. I looked from them to the not-yet converted railway-car. It had a wonderful dignity. In its austere and monumental way, it was very beautiful. It was a noble work of man, and Nature smiled on it. I wondered with what colours it was to be bejezebelled, and what name – Bolton Abbey? – Glad Eye? – Gay Wee Gehenna? – it would have to bear, and what manner of man or woman was going to rent it.

'It was on this last point that I mused especially. The housing problem is hard, doubtless; but nobody, my mind protested as I surveyed the crescent, nobody is driven to so desperate a solution of it as this! There are tents, there are caves, there are hollow trees . . . . . and there are people who prefer – this! Yes, 'this' is a positive taste, not a necessity at all.'

from 'In Homes Unblest' by Max Beerbohm in *And Even Now* (Heinemann 1920)

House-hunter (after another fruitless day). "WHAT ABOUT TAKING THIS? WE COULD AT LEAST HANG OUR PICTURES."

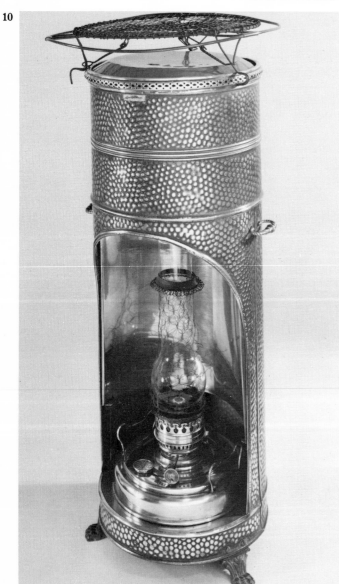

The Ardente Paraffin Room Heater at the left was an object of some importance in a 1920 home lucky enough to boast one. Throughout the winter most houses were cold, except in the kitchen during the preparation of a cooked meal or in front of the living room fire; even there, one tended to be hot at the front and cold at the back. The Ardente meant that in times of sickness the bedroom could be changed from its normal Jack-Frost-on-the-window-pane desolation to a relatively comfortable space, or that the front room could be made briefly habitable for the entertainment of an important visitor without the cost, fuss and dirt of making up a special fire.

We are, of course, here concerned with a fairly posh household. In many homes the whole of family life would be conducted around a solid fuel range – a veritable heart of the home. It made great demands on Mum who probably fed it, black leaded it and cooked on it every day of the year, but for the children it would probably always be remembered with affection as a cornucopia of delights.

Some homes enjoyed better than coal and paraffin as sources of light and heat. A more fortunate householder would have coal and gas. The most advanced homes used coal **and** gas for heat and electricity for light.

Electricity in the home was something of a rarity. The industry was supplying substantially less than a million consumers and supplies were coming through at a variety of voltages. The potential was appreciated and under the provisions of the Electricity Supply Act of 1919 five Electricity Commissioners were appointed for the purpose of promoting, regulating and supervising the supply of electricity in the United Kingdom.

The components and appliances made by the 280 manufacturers in the electrical business at that time were no more standardised than the supply. Nevertheless equipment was available and the Organisers of the Ideal Home Exhibition made some point of demonstrating the benefits that electricity could bring to the home.

The three photographs tell us a little about the period. The meal being taken (high tea?) suggests a certain formality and a conscious care for appearance in, for example, the china. This is reflected in the design of the kettle, toast rack and heating stand. We may wonder at the flex trailing up to some invisible source of power, but as late as 1934 a book on household management reassured the reader that electric irons, kettles and vacuum cleaners could 'be used from the ordinary lighting circuit, and do not require a special supply of current'.

When we move from the dining table to the kitchen the concern with appearances seems cursory. On the other hand, the placing of the equipment has a logic in terms of convenience which later generations of users, limited to mass-produced, styled and sales-orientated products, might well envy. The lady cooking by electricity is producing a joint, a pudding, boiled potatoes, fried fish cakes and apples cooked whole – with never a stoop (and has a fire extinguisher just in case of trouble). The lady with the dish-washing machine seems equally comfortable.

The electrical industry prospered during the 1920s and 1930s. The idea that manufactured power should replace human labour became a tenet of the time, though electricity was still, for many, synonymous with light. Only slowly were homes to absorb the other benefits.

11

12

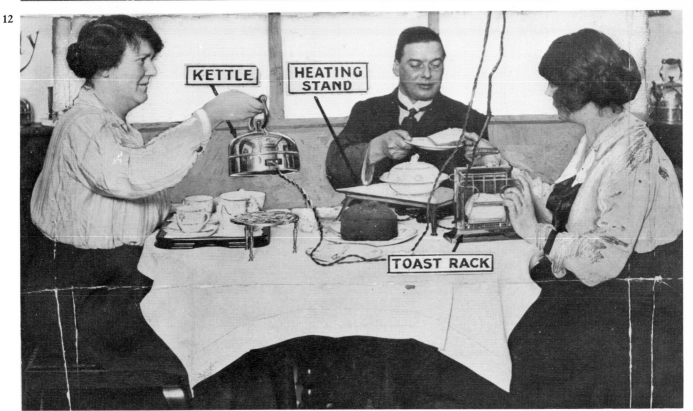

HARRODS COMPLETE £500 FLAT IN GREAT DEMAND!

Swift and enthusiastic, but hardly unexpected, has come the demand from every part of the Kingdom for details of this most attractive Harrods innovation, and already many Harrods £500 Flats are "things in being." Above is shown an illustration of the Best Bedroom.

Every essential is included for the cosy furnishing of Hall, Dining Room, Lounge-Sitting Room, Kitchen, Bathroom and Lavatory, Best Bedroom, Spare Bedroom, and Maid's Bedroom. There is also an adequate supply of Cutlery and Plate, China, Glass, Turnery, Ironmongery, and Linen.

THE BEST BEDROOM OF HARRODS £500 6-ROOM FLAT

Oak Bedroom Suite, Jacobean Design, Finished Antique Colour	£	s.	d.		£	s.	d.		£	s.	d.
6 ft. Wardrobe	34	15	0	4 ft. 6 in. Wire Spring Mattress	4	5	0	Black Iron Curb		16	9
3 ft. 6 in. Dressing Table ...	11	12	6	4 ft. 6 in. Hair and Wool Overlay Mattress ...	4	19	6	Casement Curtains and Rods	2	10	0
3 ft. 6 in. Washstand ...	7	7	0	4 ft. 6 in. Feather Bolster ...	1	5	0	Art Carpet 12 ft. by 9 ft. ...	7	17	6
Bedside Cupboard	4	0	0	2 Pillows	1	7	0				
Two Chairs (19/6 each) ...	1	19	0	Upholstered Wicker Chair...	1	17	9				
4 ft. 6 in. Oak Bedstead fitted Iron Sides, to match	8	8	0	Double Set Toilet Ware ...	1	15	0		£95	4	6
				Toilet Pail		9	6				

An attractive feature is the interchangeability of all the pieces; the Wardrobe is offered in 4 sizes, Dressing Table and Washstand in 2 sizes, Chest of Drawers in 4 sizes; any piece may be purchased separately.

A LUXURIOUS SETTEE

This Settee, from the Lounge Sitting Room of the £500 flat, is excellently upholstered, has soft loose cushions to seat, and is covered in artistic Cretonne. 5 ft. 6 in. long, Price £22.

Orders over £10 Carriage Paid to any station in Great Britain.

HARRODS
EVERYTHING FOR THE HOME

Harrods Ltd

London SW 1

Roller printed Cretonne manufactured by F. W. Grafton & Co.
/Crown Copyright, Victoria and Albert Museum

The photograph above was taken at Bournville. This Estate was started in 1879 and administered from 1900 by the Bournville Village Trust. The founder, George Cadbury, dedicated it to 'alleviating the evils which arise from the insanitary and insufficient accommodation supplied to large numbers of the working classes, and of securing to the workers in factories some of the advantages of village life.

The often repeated aims of the Trust were to build houses for the working classes, encourage gardening and create a mixed community with a communal spirit.

The Cadbury experiment was one of the great examples of industrial patronage, of which there are a number in England, and we may fairly assume the houses to incorporate every reasonable convenience in an economically self-supporting development.

So the room above represents a degree of comfort: water, gas and a bath. Even on the Bournville Estate separate bathrooms were not considered until after the Great War.

Harrods, the London store, had different priorities from Cadbury and in their immediately post-war advertisement a bathroom and a lavatory are confidently assumed. It is a mouth-watering statement of what the well-heeled home-maker could enjoy. Carriage paid, too.

CURTAINS 1920

1921

3lb self raising flour	1s 3½d
2lb granulated sugar	1s 5d
1lb cocoa	2s 10½d
20 cigarettes	11½d
1 bottle whisky	12s 6d
1 pint pale ale	8d
3 tablets toilet soap	1s 9d
400 yard reel of cotton	8d
1 yard scarlet flannel	3s 6d
10lb wedding cake	£2 2s 6d

Not everybody in England was in the plight of those soldiers who found themselves home-less when they returned to civil life. Many people inherited homes from times past – but there was considerable disparity between the quality of the inheritances.

Chequers Court, in the top picture, was presented to the nation in 1921 by Lord Lee of Fareham and became the official residence of the then and succeeding Prime Ministers. On the other hand many were living in residences typified by the lower picture, and homes of this sort were difficult to reconcile with standards of cleanliness and order which had steadily improved during the war years.

Minister of Health Christopher Addison was not only aware of the problem but deter-mined to put matters to rights. He had instructed Local Authorities to build as many homes as possible for letting at rents comparable with the 1914 level and promised Govern-ment subsidy of the greater part of the inevitable financial loss. But on 30 January 1921 the Government Finance Committee decided that there was no alternative but to decide housing questions not on merit but on financial considerations only: Addison left the Ministry in March and in July Government grants for new houses were severely limited.

The summer of 1921 was hard. Not only were the prospects of a satisfactory home for every family receding, but the unemployment doubled in the first three months of the year; in June it passed the two million mark. For those still in work wages fell heavily across the board. Salisbury's wartime Committee of the Ministry of Reconstruction had urged that it be made a duty on Local Authorities not only to make up the deficit in housing but thereafter to maintain an adequate supply.

The aspiration began to seem like pie in the sky.

'. . . . . *No one can say in his heart of hearts that London is satisfactorily housed. Charming homes there are, it is true, whether in the West End square or in the distant suburb, but none of us can shut our eyes to the miles on miles of depressing streets that lie between and make up London – not necessarily squalid, but monotonous and uninspiring to the uttermost degree.*

'*Comparatively few Londoners live in houses of which they can be reasonably proud, and only a proportion in homes with which they can be reasonably satisfied.*

'*The difficulty of finding a suitable home is one that presses upon all classes of the community. The joys of house-hunting have with all of us at some time or another been reduced to disillusionment and disappointment in the house that is found. The ideal only too often vanishes in the actual. We know exactly the house we desire, but the houses that are empty or likely to be empty all fall short in so many ways. There are frequently only to be found mouldering, mournful premises which even the enthusiasm of the house agent cannot disguise.*

'*If this is so with the houses of the comparatively well-to-do, with the working-class home it has in the past been next to impossible to exercise any choice in the quality or even in the location of the home.*

'*With the greater proportion of the population, even with increased wages, the family means are strictly limited, and in many cases the ideal of even a separate house is far beyond the attainable. Under such circumstances the conditions overpower all ideal of the home as a place of which the housewife can be proud and to which the children can in after years look back with affection.*

'. . . . *In the central areas the last thirty years have seen a steadily growing tendency to concentration in tall block dwellings or palatial hotels or flats, while simultaneously in all the suburbs there has been a steady creeping paralysis of two-story villadom, mile after mile of brick and mortar slowly eating up the countryside.*

'. . . . *The need for block dwellings arises only in comparatively few instances where it is essential to house the workers in the heart of London. Even in these cases it may be well argued that cheaper rents and healthier conditions in the suburbs more than outweigh the slight saving of time effected by living in a crowded tenement. In the one case, the whole family live perforce in crowded conditions, with scanty and cramped accommodation and at high rents, in order that the bread-winner may be near his work.*

'*The only positions where block tenements can reasonably be considered are in the rare cases where it is necessary to house workers on a particular spot of limited area. Such cases may arise in the immediate neighbourhood of the docks or in close proximity of the railway termini, but such block tenements should be discouraged as far as possible.*'

from 'The Housing of London' by W. R. Davidge, FSI in *London of the Future*
(T. Fisher Unwin 1921)

17

" MY DEAR, I'VE BOUGHT THE VERY PLACE TO SHOW OFF OUR FURNITURE—A REALLY FINE JACOBETHIAN MANSION."

‘Harebell’ Roller printed cotton designed by Minnie McLeish.
/*Crown Copyright, Victoria and Albert Museum*

These three interiors are more of Bournville. It seems unlikely that the furnishings were purchased at Harrods, but they do relate nicely to the advertisement on page 12. They seem to represent comfortable home norms of the early twenties. Both the living room and bedroom are equipped with orderly, decent and yet strangely negative furniture. In it one can detect references to styles long gone, and to high style of the immediate past. The references, however, are so remote from their sources, so pale a reflection, that the furniture takes on its own period identity and the pieces sit easily together in calm disregard of current fashion.

The extremes of 1921 varied from the ‘Jacobethan’ excesses noted by *Punch* to a considerable vogue for the exotic expressed with particular reference to China and the Chinoiserie of the eighteenth century. The success of a few complete Chinese Rooms created for the fashionable and rich led to a crop of occasional items destined to sit uncomfortably (and often unused) in many a modest home. However, within a year, just as the followers of fashion were feeling in touch with the leaders, the excavation of Tutankh-Amen's tomb at Thebes ruined everything. Fabrics and furniture suddenly needed an Egyptian flavour!

CURTAINS 1921

1922

These two lucky children of 1922 not only have a train but also a home on the Becontree Estate, one of the London County Council's major housing schemes. Elsewhere frustration was turning to anger about the failure of Britain to find homes for its onetime heroes. Whilst 80,000 houses were built during the year under the provisions for subsidy to local authorities who put the work in hand, this represented simply the completion of jobs started earlier and there were no new provisions for a continuity of such subsidies.

The Director General of Housing, representing the Government, claimed that houses which cost £816 in 1921 were in 1922 being built for £300. The National Federation of House Builders refuted this statement, saying that the comparison was not between the same classes of house at all.

Certainly material costs had fallen in the twelve months up to April 1922. Cement had fallen from 80s a ton to 63s; stock bricks from over 100s to 82s, one-inch flooring boards from 40s per standard to 30s 6d.

There were clearly some reductions in house prices. Alas, local authorities were reluctant to continue building houses in the absence of Government subsidy and the potential private home builder was more often than not waiting for prices to fall further before investing in his own place. There were some self-congratulatory comments to the effect that post-war housing had been an aesthetic and social success; it was generally agreed that the subsidised housing schemes had resulted in a better home for the working man's family than had ever, with few exceptions, been achieved before; it was claimed that the lucky occupants were feeling a pride in their homes which was a new and doubtless pleasing experience. But the unhappy truth was that the deficit in houses had risen from some 600,000 houses at the armistice to over 800,000 in 1922.

'*To The Editor of* The New Statesman

Sir, – I should like to confirm what your correspondent says as to the disadvantage of gas heating.
"In warm or temperate weather it is almost ideal. But whenever there is a cold spell it breaks
down" – and has to be supplemented with oil stoves. In one respect my experience differs from
that of "C.D.S." We do get hot baths from our geyser, but although it was fixed, approved and
repeatedly inspected by the Gas Company, it gives off with the hot water such suffocating fumes
that windows and doors have to be opened, and no one can remain in the bathroom while the hot
water is running.

'*I have also tried electric stoves, and find that they dim the light and are continually breaking*
down if more than one is used in the house at the same time, apparebtly because the cables are
not strong enough to bear the extra load, although the Electric Light Company continues ener-
getically to advertise these stoves and to instal them at great expense and (like the gas company)
without warning the consumer of their disadvantages.

'*I do not sign my name, as I do not want to be visited by a succession of inspectors and man-*
agers who will tell me politely that their service is quite perfect –
Yours etc., J. M.'

from *The New Statesman* (28 January 1922)

22

THE DAWN OF SPRING IN OUR SUBURB.
STUDY OF TWO ROMANTIC NATURES RISING SUPERIOR TO THEIR ENVIRONMENT.

Music was and had always been an ingredient of family life. A piano was often regarded as a necessity of civilised life rather than a luxury. Whilst many a child suffered agonies once a week at the piano lesson many a home was illuminated by the family sharing an evening of music making.

The gramophone, which came into being during the 19th Century, made a musical evening much more simple though the ease of making music merely by winding a handle was often deplored as destructive of some of the best qualities of shared relaxation. By 1922 the manufacture of gramophones was so sophisticated that it was even possible to conceive of – and make – an object with the threefold purpose of being 'an artistic lamp, a provider of music and a decorative item'.

Bur now family parties could enjoy a new delight called wireless.

Interest had been aroused when the *Daily Mail* sponsored a wireless concert of songs by Dame Nellie Melba from the Marconi Works on 16 June, 1920; it intensified when, in 1922, the British Broadcasting Company was formed and was given a monopoly of transmission in Britain. Broadcasts from Marconi House started on 14 November.

There was an All-British Wireless Exhibition at the Horticultural Hall in London during October. Madam Tetrazzini listened to and purchased a set. Heals, the famous London furniture store, made a splendid cabinet for the British Broadcasting Company to present to King George V and schoolboys all over the nation were busily making simple 'crystal sets' through which, on a good day, sounds could indeed be heard.

Nor was it only schoolboys who made sets. The fact that the BBC was originally financed by a group of manufacturers in no way deterred the ingenious family from making its own receiver. Reception was not always good, but a pair of headphones (often shared by two heads locked together by an arc of metal) gave a new dimension to life in the home.

A licence fee was required of all owners of a receiver and for that fee the manager of the BBC, John Reith, was determined to provide 'all that was best in every department of human knowledge, endeavours and achievement'.

WIRELESS AS A MEANS OF EDUCATING THE MUSICAL TASTE OF CHILDREN. A HAPPY FAMILY PARTY LISTENING-IN TO AN OPERA.

Block printed chintz.
/*Crown Copyright, Victoria and Albert Museum*

The lady, her cat and her dog, photographed in 1922, are living in a converted railway arch at Harrow.

The location is unusual but the furnishings conform. Less has been spent on the bedroom than the living room. The cast iron bedstead, wardrobe and chair are quite likely second-hand. The dressing table and washhand stand are clearly home-made. As a contemporary advertisement explained, 'Knowing how to do "odd jobs" and repairs, and how to make things for the home, means the saving of expense in many directions. Most men could be handymen but lack the necessary knowledge. *Work* is a long established weekly which supplies this knowledge in a simple straight-forward manner'.

Cost saving was one necessity, space saving another. Convertible, adjustable and reducible furniture was the order of the day. The more ingenious the piece the more it was likely to sell (though often enough the less its flexibility was likely to be exploited).

In the living room under the railway arch the space occupied by the gate leg table top is splendidly variable.

However, for really dashing flexibility it would be hard to beat the bath above, complete with drainage, kept in a kitchen cupboard.

CURTAINS 1922

The drawings above are from a book published by Duckworth & Co in 1923 under the title *The House We Ought to Live In*. Whilst only a very few people could aspire to the luxury it describes, it was felt that the lucky occupants of new homes generally were enjoying much improved standards of accommodation.

The *British Builder* commented that new housing schemes had 'produced a better class of workman's dwellings than had (with few exceptions) existed in this country before and created in the tenant a pride in his home which was, perhaps, a somewhat new and pleasing experience'.

Developments which appeared unquestionably to support this contention were careful selection of building sites; smaller groups of houses in place of long terraces; better planning and lighting of better-sized rooms; improved sanitation – including a WC for every home where water supply was available and the limitation, imposed in 1921, of a maximum of 12 houses to the acre. The impact of this last provision can be appreciated if one compares the resulting accommodation of 50 or 60 people on an acre of land with the 330 living on a similar area in Shoreditch at the time. For them there was no immediate transformation of a gloomy scene.

A 1923 Act of Parliament did provide for limited state assistance to local authorities and, through the authorities, to the private enterprise builders of homes. The provision, originally limited to houses completed by 1925, was extended to cover those completed by 1939 and throughout that period the struggle to help the badly housed was continued.

The principle that the housing of those who could not afford the market price should be a social service was accepted and, as *Punch* notes in his cartoon, the retail trade was getting round to a less charitable method of helping those who were short of cash.

'*Now that the speculative builder is at work again houses are to be had, though the demand is much greater than the supply. But those who have a small capital can at least buy a roof to shelter them. The prospect is no longer so hopeless as once it was. Thanks to private enterprise, at last able to enter the field, estates are springing up on the outskirts of London which promise to meet an urgent need.*

'*That the speculator has been obliged to go out into the country where the air is fresh and the prospect pleasing is matter for congratulation. The movement of the townspeople outwards makes for health. For this contribution to the problem of London's congestion we must all be grateful. But while the enterprise of the speculative builder has its good points there are unfortunately also reasons for grave disquiet. He is certainly giving us houses, but we are not getting homes.*

'*Alluring brochures describe the beauties and conveniences of many new estates around London, with the* rus in urbe *appeal so dear to the heart of the modern suburban couple. But a tour of some of the new estates suggests that care must be taken that we do not get all the old faults of the pre-war middle-class house repeated.*

'*. . . . We went into a typical new 'villa' the other day. The rooms were small. The largest was not more than 12ft by 10ft. The hall was described as a "lounge hall", but it opened right on to the porch. The kitchen was not big enough for a good-sized table, and there was no scullery. Nor was there a copper. Assuming that the owners would have a servant, which is almost certain, the absence of a scullery is a grave defect. The kitchen is the maid's living-room, and should be designed with that fact in view.*

'*. . . . We found the stairs deep and winding, perilous for children and tiring for adults. The main criticism of the bedroom floor is that the bathroom was ridiculously small. In one case the door could not be opened to the full extent because the lavatory basin stopped it. Electric light was laid on, but there were no power plugs.*

'*This is a fair sample of the sort of "villa" which is today being built for a little over a thousand pounds, or on easy terms, with interest, about twelve hundred and fifty.*

'*No house was equipped for central heating. None had adequate cupboard accommodation. None had enough fittings. They certainly had dressers with glass doors, but nowhere did we find a kitchen cabinet such as the housewife gets in America. In no case were there any basins with hot and cold water fitted in the bedrooms. Beyond the mantel-pieces there were no permanent fitments in the two main rooms downstairs, and no built-in wardrobe in the hall, which in most cases was a waste of valuable space for the sake of vanity.*

'*This sort of thing will not do.*'

from 'Houses – But No Homes' by Crossley Davies in the *Architects' Journal* (7 February 1923)

32

Bride (*showing the new house*). "AND HOW DO YOU LIKE OUR FURNITURE, AUNT? WE'RE GETTING IT ON THE INSTALMENT PLAN, YOU KNOW."
Aunt. "IT'S NOT BAD; BUT PERHAPS I SHALL LIKE THE SECOND INSTALMENT BETTER."

Everything that the heart of the home-lover could wish for is to be found at Hampton's, Pall Mall East. They have recently opened a new department in which colour is the chief consideration. No matter what the colour scheme of a room may be, Hampton's can provide the right cushions, lamp-shades, rugs, and furniture to harmonise with it.

Whilst John Gloag was describing the house his contemporaries ought to live in, many who had no choice were trying to decide how to furnish the homes they were really going to occupy.

Between the extremes of Tut-ankh-Amen (already a shade passé) and Jacobethan there were alternatives.

The lady on the page opposite seems already in her daydream comfortably settled amongst the years fashionable furnishings available in Hampton's Store. Had she been more concerned to furnish with equipment which was beautifully made and likely to continue to satisfy her when the novelty had worn off, she might have done better to invest in the furniture illustrated on this page and made by Gordon Russell in his new factory at Broadway, Worcs.

Russell was wholly antagonistic to ephemeral pastiche and shoddy manufacture. He extended the best traditions of English furniture-making through the inter-war years and applied the craftsman's disciplines and skills to factory production.

By his talent and integrity as designer and maker he realised in practice the appeal of the then very active Design and Industries Association that people should consider 'Fitness for purpose' the criteria for objects they made, sold, bought and used. The Association's national concern was generally overwhelmed by the fashionable influences of the time: Gordon Russell was not.

35

A Double Bedroom with a hanging recess and fitted cupboards

The Kitchen showing cooker and tradesmen's door

The Study

'Little flower' Block printed cotton by Dorothy Larcher.
/*Bath Crafts Study Centre Collection*

Gloag's house we ought to live in was created with architect Leslie Mansfield and illustrated by A. B. Read, who later achieved eminence as a designer.

With hindsight one may think the suggestions neither adventurous nor stimulating, but in 1923 many a home-maker would be delighted by a feast of thoughtful ideas suitable not only to a new home but capable also of introduction into an existing shell. Built-in bedroom furniture could be a revelation; even shelves either side of the study fireplace might be seen as a startling innovation. The kitchen table with different surfaces for different jobs, the hinged flap by the cooker and the aide-memoire above would all appeal as important contributions to a well-appointed home.

In any event the rooms are laudable applications of the DIA's Fitness for purpose dicta and a wholesome alternative to promptings in some monthly magazines concerned with the home. Silver ceilings, black walls and other dramas were rather more simple to copy than to live with.

Gloag campaigned continuously for more sensible standards in our environment. He identified the period as the age of amateur decorators; he frequently addressed himself to them and was often understood.

CURTAINS 1923

1924

1924
3lb self raising flour	10½d
2lb granulated sugar	1s 3½d
1lb cocoa	2s 4½d
1lb Indian tea	3s 4d
20 cigarettes	11½d
1 bottle whisky	12s 6d
1 pint pale ale	7d
3 tablets toilet soap	1s 6d
1 yard scarlet flannel	3s 4d
10lb wedding cake	£1 17s 0d

40

In 1924 the Northern Line of the London Underground railway system was extended to Edgware. One picture above shows the terminal station in course of construction in 1923. The lower picture is of the same area some years later.

Examples of this sort can be cited over the length and breadth of the land. It is characteristic of how an extended public transport system encouraged long-distance commuting and an explosion of building at the periphery of major and developing towns. Reaching even further into the countryside than the London Underground system, the main-line railways seem often to have been developed with the separation of place of work and home as a positively desirable criteria. The extension and electrification of the Southern Railway in the 1920s is a case in point. At the other extreme an expansion of bus and tram services provided short-distance commuting much more conveniently than the horse omnibus of pre-war years. As a result, by the end of the 1930s an area of something like 15 miles from the centre of London was blanketed over by houses built at 12 or 14 to the acre.

Many, many families were enamoured of the idea of escaping from their urban homes into the country. The air would be more healthy, the moral atmosphere would be improved, the anonymous monotony of urban terraces, which paradoxically sometimes supported a feeling of isolation, would give way to happier societies in which the house itself would express individuality and reinforce the 'sense of home'.

These were not new thoughts. Ebenezer Howard had written at the turn of the century 'Town and Country must be married and out of this joyous union will spring a new hope, a new life and a new civilisation'.

Improved transport facilities transformed this ideal into a tangible possibility.

41

UNDERGROUND

LEAVE THIS AND

'I never had any other desire so strong and so like to covetousness as that one which I have had always, that I might be Master of a small House and a Large Garden, with moderate conveniences joined to them.'

MOVE TO EDGWARE

'*Letter to the Editor of* Country Life

'*Sir – The village is small and old and any new building immediately attracts our attention and criticism. For several weeks they have been erecting two small cottages at the end of our Chief Street, and yesterday they began to put on the roofs. They are actually using slates.*

'*Now, the chance traveller will walk down the row of white-walled, thatch-crowned cottages and will just be growing interested in their old world atmosphere when he will suddenly be confronted by the uninspired grey of the new slates. Surely, there is enough dirty-red brick and slate-grey drabness in towns and cities without there being any necessity to tamper with what few untouched hamlets we have remaining. The thatch roof is not only picturesque, but exceedingly useful. Thatching is almost a lost art. Yet comfort is much greater under thatch than under a slate roof, as anyone who has lived in a thatched roofed house will tell you; for thatch keeps out the cold in winter and, paradoxically enough, prevents undue heat in summer. The fact is, machinery is gradually killing thatching. Nowadays we have machines to prepare the straw for thatched roof, and machine-made thatch is not so durable as that prepared by hand. A hand-thatched roof will last about 25 years and costs about 3d or 4d a square foot. Thatch which is machine-manufactured while, perhaps, being a little cheaper, will decay long before the period elapses, and it is this quicker decay which is making slate roofs more common in villages. After continually patching his roof the average villager will replace his machine-prepared thatch with wood or slates. Many people seem to be influenced by the generally accepted idea that thatch is inflammable; yet, while loose, dry straw is quickly ignited and burns rapidly, tightly packed straw or thatch burns very slowly and produces more smoke than flame. Slowly the old thatched roofs are disappearing and the more modern slate is successfully invading our village. When this invasion is complete, I suppose, we shall still be able to view a specimen of real thatch in our museums.*
F. W.

from *Country Life* (26 April 1924)

42

Long-suffering Husband. "I SAY, MONICA, DO LET'S LEAVE CHELSEA AND SIT ON CHAIRS AGAIN."

1028   **Army and Navy Co-operative Society, Ltd.**   Deptl. Enquiries) 345
Telephone No. ¦

43

SPECIAL RUSTIC ARCHES (Peeled, Stained and Varnished).

No. 15. Flat Top.   No. 13. Round Top.   No. 16. Flat Gothic Top.   No. 14. Double Top.

Each .... 22/9   Each .... 23/6   Each .... 21/3   Each 27/6

These Arches are made of selected material, and are strongly built. Made in sections. Height, 9 ft. 6 in., allowing for 1 ft. 6 in. in ground and 8 ft. above ground when fixed. Width across path, 4 ft.

NOTE.—These can also be supplied in a cheaper quality, with rustic wood in a natural state. Prices on application.

Rustic Rose Pillar.

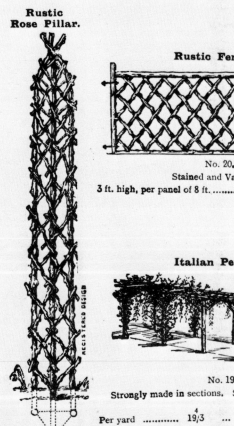

Rustic Fencing.

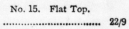

No. 20.

Stained and Varnished.

3 ft. high, per panel of 8 ft. .... each 25/6

Pigeon Cote.

Rustic Rose Pole.

Italian Pergola.

No. 19.

Strongly made in sections. Stained and Varnished.

Per yard .... 19/3 ... 22/6 ... 6 ft. across path. 25/6

No. 35.

Stained and Varnished.

6 hole	....	55/0
12 ,,	....	96/3
18 ,,	....	136/3
24 ,,	....	181/6

Pole and Spurs, 24/3 extra.

No. 17.

Well and strongly made. Stained and Varnished. 10 ft. out of ground when fixed.

Each 24/0

No. 18.

Strongly made. Stained and Varnished.

10 ft. out of ground when fixed.

Each 17/3

Particulars of other Designs and Estimates for Rustic Work of every description to be had on application.

NOTE.—Sent direct from Works, Carriage not paid.

ALL PRICES ARE SUBJECT TO MARKET FLUCTUATIONS.

Did Monica leave page 31 and Chelsea for a flat in conventional Belgravia or go by Underground, to a house with a garden? We shall never know. We do know that thousands confirmed Baldwin's view that the English will have a tiny bit of garden if they can.

Its use was a matter for family decision. A garden, tended by a dedicated vegetable grower like the gentleman on his plot, could make a very important contribution to balancing the household budget. It is easy to imagine his satisfaction as he cut a cabbage or gathered a basket of apples. Other families, perhaps financially better endowed, made personal pleasure grounds. The only unusual thing about seeing the vegetable gardeners plot cheek-by-jowl with a garden like that above would be the coincidence of finding two such accomplished gardening families living in neighbouring homes.

The style of a garden mattered little to the suppliers of seeds, plants and garden equipment. The magazines declared the job for the week, the suppliers' advertisements defined the right materials and everything in the business seemed lovely. The Army and Navy Stores Catalogue 1924-25 carried 48 pages on the subject. The gardener must have been transported by the prospects before him. A gothic-topped rustic arch, or a flat top? or should one spend a few coppers more and have a round top?

44

45

Roller printed cotton.
/*Crown Copyright, Victoria and Albert Museum*

The occupier of a new suburban home looking over the barren expanse of his surrounding territory would readily imagine a transformation into something like the picture above. Unfortunately, as V. S. Solly was to write during the 1920s: 'a kind of hysteria seems apt to possess the pioneers of a newly developed suburb'.

The hysteria was particularly apparent in the garden. Questions of appropriate scale, neighbourliness and convenience gave way to an illogical romanticism which as often as not suggested that if an Englishman's home was his castle his garden was his Municipal park.

No matter. Many a family new to the suburbs, freed from the restraints of a window box or the confines of a paved back yard, found an earthly paradise. The gardens on the page opposite, verdant and cared for, reveal a passionate interest in the undertaking.

And perhaps for the first time Mother had a place to hang the washing and to take the air, children had a space to play outdoors and Father, when the tools were put away, could contemplate with some real satisfaction an achievement which linked his property to the great English gardens and associate himself with the great Gardeners.

CURTAINS 1924

House building was often inhibited in the early 1920s by a shortage of materials and skilled labour. In the south-east, particularly, bricks were often hard to come by; and to add to the problems it was said that brickies were laying as few as 300 bricks per day compared with a thousand and more before the war. By 1925 Architect Manning Robertson was able to state definitely that brick was, and seemed likely to remain, the most generally satisfactory material for building houses. He was, however, constrained to add that 'supplementary methods have their place.'

A lot of effort went into investigating these methods. Nothing came of Neville Chamberlain's political musing that paper houses would be ideal if they were waterproof and warm and could be destroyed when they became insanitary, but as early as 1922 the *Daily Mail* had sponsored a village of 41 cottages using 16 different systems of construction. The top picture shows a pair of steel houses which hit the news in November of 1925, when the Duke of Atholl was present to explain points of interest to enquirers and critics. The lower shows other experimental houses at Bournville. Little came of the experiments. They were on too small a scale to reveal economies and were often abrogated by restrictive and obsolete bye-laws. However, it is possible that the most powerful deterrent to pioneers was the conflict between a general wish for variety and distinction between homes and the degree of standardisation needed to justify the new building methods.

Furthermore, however novel the structure, and in spite of a demand for smaller, convenient, labour-saving homes, there seems always to have been a feeling the house should simulate a traditional and conventional home both as to arrangement and appearance. That disposition was to change radically in a decade or so.

'It is usually supposed that village life in England is much superior to town life in certain most vital concerns – especially in health and morals.

'. . . . . In some respects the countryman today is worse than he was in the 13th Century. They were then careful of their teeth, and were in the habit of cleaning them with twigs of trees from which the bark was freshly pulled. Today the tooth brush is scarcely known.

'. . . . The lack of cottages of any decent size leads, as the word suggests, to gross indecency. Families with insufficient room for themselves are under great pressure to take in lodgers, generally young or middle-aged men who have work in or about the village, but have no sort of chance of getting a cottage or even a single room to themselves.

'Instances are legion in which these lodgers sleep in the same room with various members of the family, more or less independent of considerations of age and sex. It would serve no good purpose to give examples of the indecencies, not to say scandals, that result.

'They have come into the open or have been more widely realised by the people who have better houses and more elbow room to be decent in, owing to the pension officers, whose business it has been to look into the moral and physical well-being of children and widows and, less often, of the ill or disabled ex-service men themselves.

'The greater leniency of the officials to widowed beneficiaries who have transgressed the moral code is doubtless due in fact to the perception of the difficulties of life in villages, where the people are too many for the houses. Ii has come to be a sort of standard of conduct that one illegitimate child is allowable, but that two is not respectable.'

from *John Bull* (1925)

52

Visitor. "WHAT A LOVELY OLD FIREPLACE!"
Owner. "YES, GENUINE ELIZABETHAN. HAD IT PUT IN. MUST MOVE WITH THE TIMES, YOU KNOW."

An experimental steel house was on display at the 1925 British Industries Fair. The illustration shows the scullery with the bathroom beyond. It is difficult to understand how such important spaces could be dealt with in so cavalier a manner; how little attention was paid to the comfort and convenience of service areas!

The kitchen, even in homes which did not include a Maid's Room, had not received the careful thought of either supplier or user that was to come. Perhaps user is the wrong word. Servants were not the privilege only of the very rich and there were still housewives who had little concern with the kitchen other than giving instructions. Whilst many women suffered as a drudge in their own homes, a sizeable and influential minority found bridge, teashops and good works a necessary aid to passing the time between hubby's departure for work and his return.

The domestic servant joke was a staple of that careful and accurate commentator on the inter-war years, *Punch*. Even the joke of 1939 on page 123 gratuitously includes a uniformed maid and a gardener as normal to a suburban home.

Nevertheless there was, through the two decades, an inexorable reduction in the number of people engaged in private service. There were many reasons.

Domestic Service was a less attractive prospect than it had been before the newly rich employers of the nineteenth century had substituted 'lower orders' for friendly helpers. The job was often lonely and boring. Many girls were more attracted to working in industry, in an office or behind the counter in a shop. This diversity of opportunity had

greatly increased since women's involvement in various jobs, previously though to be male prerogatives, during the Great War.

At the same time even the rich, troubled by rising costs and taxes, found it necessary or convenient to reduce their household establishments. Aside from strictly practical considerations there was a growing sense of guilt about class, wealth and poverty. During times of depression, when many might have enjoyed a leisurely life at home whilst at the same time helping others with comfortable employment, the arrangement seemed socially dubious. A stigma attached both to employing servants and being servants; resentment between the parties was not unknown.

Not that there was a sudden revolution. At the outbreak of the Second World War many homes were paying a salary of little more than a pound a week and 'all found' to a general servant who could well have worn a uniform not unlike those illustrated in the 1925 edition of the Army and Navy Stores Catalogue.

More often service would be provided by a 'Daily', 'Weekly' or 'Treasure' who augmented her own housekeeping money with a few shillings from the lady of the slightly more prosperous home. Happily those arrangements tended to be of a sort in which social distinctions were broken down in cheerful collaboration rather than emphasised to demonstrate egregious superiority.

54

682   *Army and Navy Co-operative Society, Ltd.*   Deptl. Enquiries ⎫ 92
                                                             Telephone No. ⎭

MAIDS' CAPS AND APRONS

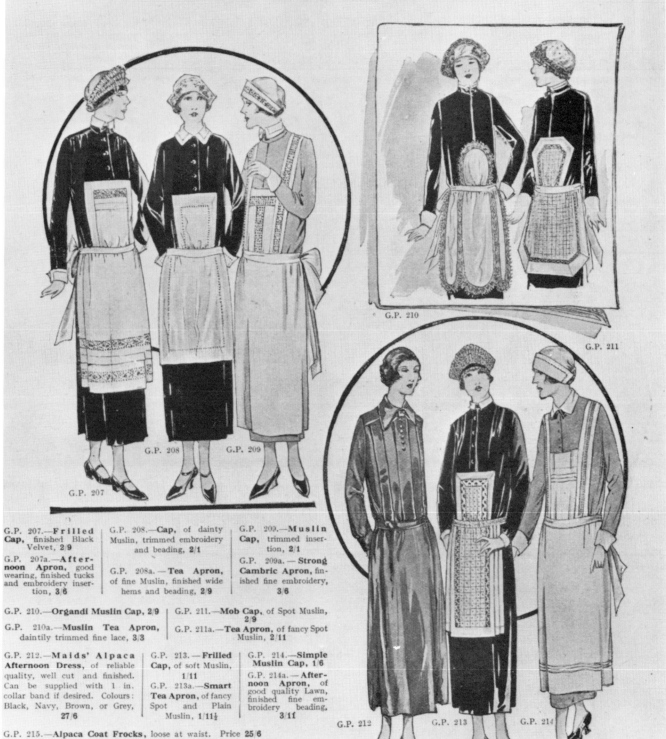

G.P. 210

G.P. 211

G.P. 207

G.P. 208   G.P. 209

G.P. 212   G.P. 213   G.P. 214

G.P. 207.—Frilled Cap, finished Black Velvet, 2/9

G.P. 207a.—Afternoon Apron, good wearing, finished tucks and embroidery insertion, 3/6

G.P. 208.—Cap, of dainty Muslin, trimmed embroidery and beading, 2/1

G.P. 208a. — Tea Apron, of fine Muslin, finished wide hems and beading, 2/9

G.P. 209.—Muslin Cap, trimmed insertion, 2/1

G.P. 209a. — Strong Cambric Apron, finished fine embroidery, 3/6

G.P. 210.—Organdi Muslin Cap, 2/9

G.P. 210a.—Muslin Tea Apron, daintily trimmed fine lace, 3/3

G.P. 211.—Mob Cap, of Spot Muslin, 2/9

G.P. 211a.—Tea Apron, of fancy Spot Muslin, 2/11

G.P. 212.—Maids' Alpaca Afternoon Dress, of reliable quality, well cut and finished. Can be supplied with 1 in. collar band if desired. Colours: Black, Navy, Brown, or Grey, 27/6

G.P. 213. — Frilled Cap, of soft Muslin, 1/11

G.P. 213a.—Smart Tea Apron, of fancy Spot and Plain Muslin, 1/11½

G.P. 214.—Simple Muslin Cap, 1/6

G.P. 214a.—Afternoon Apron, of good quality Lawn, finished fine embroidery beading, 3/11

G.P. 215.—Alpaca Coat Frocks, loose at waist. Price 25/6

G.P. 216.—Maids' Morning Dresses of strong Washing Gingham, with Peter Pan collar or 1 in. collar band, in Blue, Grey, Butcher, or Steel. Price 12/11

Sizes	Waist.	Skirt Length.	Sizes	Waist.	Skirt Length.
.. ..	26 in.	32 in.	..	28 in.	36 in.
,, ..	26 ,,	34 ,,	,, ...	30 ,,	38 ,,

ALL PRICES ARE SUBJECT TO MARKET FLUCTUATIONS

Block printed linen by Gregory Brown.
/*Crown Copyright, Victoria and Albert Museum*

We can be fairly certain the photograph above shows a room as it was in 1925. It was taken in 1924 – at 84 Dover House Road on the London County Council's new housing estate. It reveals eloquently what must be the home of a mature working class couple – re-housed and bringing with them some of their 'bits and pieces' from the old home. Kitchen, dining and sitting room combined, it has a fireplace fitted with a solid fuel range. This provided not only a fire to sit by, but hot-plate, oven and possibly boiler for hot water supply as well. It was the hub of daily life – source of a good deal of pride and object of a good deal of attention, with 'Zebra' blacking, emery paper or 'Brasso' polish for iron, steel and brass parts respectively.

The 'Lady of the House' at No 84 was likely to be the 'Daily' in another household, where the eating arrangements might be more like those in the dining rooms opposite. Their exact dates are unknown, but the mirrors over the mantelpiece and the pendant corona and flounce light fittings are characteristic of the early and mid-1920s. Three things distinguish the later room: the electric power socket in the skirting; the lightness and elegance of the furniture and the built-in service hatch – a compensation, no doubt for the lack of butler or maid.

CURTAINS 1925

The upper picture shows a house which by 1926 had been a home for hundreds of years. Comfortably settled on its site, it enjoys an easy and seemingly inevitable integration with its garden.

The lower photograph shows a house in Northampton named 'Newways', completed in 1926 to the design of German Architect Peter Behrens. It is probably the first manifestation in England of a home designed in a manner which had by then gained some currency in other European countries.

There were many people eager to condemn what they saw as an unsuitable foreign fashion or style. 'Progressive' architects and their sympathisers would resist any suggestion that the new architecture was a style at all. They would argue that it was a result of designing logically to provide an environment suited to the life of the times.

Certainly Newways is not deeply rooted in national character. It sits uneasily in its grounds and makes no concession, except that of size, to the neighbouring houses.

The grounds seen in the photograph are something left over from a previous home on the site. The owner of the new house had it in mind to make changes, giving a greater conformity between house and garden.

Whatever the neighbours and the nation thought, the influences of this new way of thinking were to be strongly felt in England during the 1930s – particularly in the interiors of existing homes, where logic and simplicity could be enjoyed without having to give outward recognition of new and possibly disturbing brooms within.

Indeed the dicthotomy between Newways and its site had some of the elements of a splendid English compromise – a bright, modern, easily maintained set of rooms surrounded by a romantic, picturesque early English garden.

'It is generally conceded that the electrical millennium is about due in 15 years time, and, without stretching the imagination to breaking point, one may safely visualise some remarkable developments in town and country, in the home and the factory.

'Today perhaps one home in 20 is lighted by electricity. In 1940 the electric light will be universal, with all that it means in cleanliness and health. Homes, too, will be electrically warmed, chimneys will be out of date, and the smoke of the domestic hearth only a memory of the past.

'Moreover, the long, toilsome day of the "busy housewife" will be past, and the health and physique of the children will be greatly improved because their mothers will have more time and patience to attend to their needs. Washing, drying, ironing, and cooking will lose their terrors. The mangle and the sewing machine will be electrically driven. Even stairs may become obsolete, for the electric lift will be a commonplace even in small houses and a necessity in large ones.

'Even the domestic broom will give place everywhere to the vacuum cleaner and dust will disappear like magic, to the great advantage of health and the suppression of infection. Even the fly plague will be exorcised by the same means, whilst with the easy and effective sterilisation of water and milk another nail will be driven into the coffin of a high death rate, and the span of life taken an unprecedented rise. Thus it is quite possible that a large percentage of babies born in 1940 will live to see 2040.

'It may not be true even in 1940 that the baby will be electronically bathed, but at least the smallest cottage will have its regular supply of electrically heated water, available at any hour of day and night . . . . .'

from *Tit-Bits* (13 February 1926)

60

New Maid (*emerging from service-hatch*). "Do I have to come through this hole every time?"

61

62

63

44

'Lyon' Block printed cotton by Phyllis Barron and Dorothy Larcher.
/*Bath Crafts Study Centre Collection*

W. J. Basset-Lowke, a practical man with a passion for mechanical efficiency (he was founder of a famous firm of model railway engineers), spared no effort to achieve rational planning and efficient services in his new house Newways; rain water was drained internally from the flat roof to a soft water storage tank; service pipes and electric wiring were ducted for easy maintenance. He wished his adventurous concern for convenience and comfort to be expressed visually, internally no less than externally.

The major entertaining rooms [three of which, the dining room, hall and lounge, are shown at the left] were the work of Peter Behrens, the architect. The house was centrally heated, but a coal fire was introduced (the *Architectural Review* tells us) 'on account of its sentimental value and human appeal'. There was something else arranged for sentimental reasons. Basset-Lowke contrived the decoration of his study, shown above, to be a reproduction of the hall in his earlier house. This had been designed by C. R. Mackintosh, an architect of the Art Nouveau Movement.

It is a delight to show in a review of the 1920s and 1930s some work of Mackintosh, a man recognised in his time in Europe, though much later in Britain for his creative genius. For once perhaps the 'repro' game was justified.

CURTAINS 1926

1927

3lb self raising flour	11½d
2lb granulated sugar	8d
1lb cocoa	2s
1lb Indian tea	3s
20 cigarettes	11½d
1 bottle whisky	12s 6d
1 pint pale ale	7d
3 tablets toilet soap	1s 6d
400 yard reel of cotton	5d
1 yard scarlet flannel	3s 6d
10lb wedding cake	£1 12s 6d

Even the pleasures of a comfortable home could occasionally pall.

'Getting away from it all' was a recurring topic of conversation during the inter-war years, and the car was often the means of satisfying the urge. During these 21 years the number of motor cars registered in Britain increased tenfold, from less than 200,000 to to nearly 2 million.

As early as 1927 a drive in the car had become more than a rich man's pleasure. People of ordinary means found it possible to commute to work, even where no public transport was available, and so could move freely from a home in the country to work in the towns. Although there must have been few who wished to do the reverse, there were some working in the towns who were enabled to escape from the restricted urban life of the working week on a weekend outing to the delights of the countryside. In 1922 Sir Herbert Austin had brought out a seven horsepower car which became known as the Austin Chummy or the Baby Austin; a modest sober little car, which in 1927 cost from £135. It was so popular it inevitably became the subject of much comment from contemporary humorists. It was described as the 'baby' whose garage supplanted the nursery in middle-class homes. Perhaps this was not so flippant a joke as it seems. Maybe there were many newly married couples, encouraged by Dr Marie Stopes' campaign for birth control and informed by her book *Married Love* (published in 1926 and which ran into ten editions), who pondered carefully which baby should come first. When buying the 'semi' it became important to make sure that, even if there were no garage, there was at least space to build one between your pair and the next.

Of course the car was blamed for some deteriorations in family life. On a fine Sunday morning the Vicar would note a distinct reduction of the size of his congregation. Parents worried about their sons driving too fast on dangerous roads in a suspect second-hand car 'bought for a song', whilst their neighbours would be worrying more about his girl friend – their daughter – 'parked' with him in the moonlight, up some secluded lane.

'. . . . . Our own houses have great charm, for either they are old farmhouses or cottages adapted to our need or they are mansions designed by artists, and so we take tea together on our trimmed lawns or under our old oak beams and are all very indignant or superior about the ugly little houses that stare at us as we go by, not unlike rather pugnacious poor relations who have been invited for once to a grand party. But there are other people here – people we do not ask to tea, of course – who are happy and excited about those houses. They sit up at night wondering if they can afford to live in one of them. For years now, you see, they have been living with the wife's father or the husband's brother, crowded into a couple of tiny rooms, perhaps, and it has all been very uncomfortable and there have been little quarrels and they have not been able to ask their friends when they would have liked to, and when the husband was down with 'flu or the wife was having another baby it was so bad that life hardly seemed worth living. And now they may be able to have a place of their own, a lovely place with a proper sink in and a sort of bath in the kitchen, if it will only run to it. So they go and look over those new houses, seeing them as a kind of signpost pointing to a sunlit main road of life; while the rest of us, fortunate or cunning enough to have installed ourselves snugly and picturesquely, hurry past the ugly little brick boxes to ask the Vicar's wife or Major Brown if it really is not too bad and if something cannot be done about it.

'Even a local builder, you will notice, can suddenly turn our minds into a battlefield, where a desire for beauty wars our common human sympathy. A few more of these houses and this place will not longer charm the eye; a great many more of them and it will be hideous; but on the other hand a number of people will have the chance at last of living decently and in comfort. The thorough-going aesthete, who admits to caring for nothing but his own exquisite sensations, would have the landscape unspoilt though the remaining cottages should be crammed with wretched fellow creatures. The rest of us, not being made of such hard glittering stuff, cannot help feeling that people should come first, that their chunks of happiness or misery are more important than certain delicate satisfactions of our own: and it seems to us that the other way of thinking is like refusing to save a man's life because he has a detestably ugly face. We should be content to make the whole country hideous if we know for certain that by doing so we could also make all the people in it moderately happy'.

from 'Houses' by J. B. Priestley in *The Saturday Review* (11 June 1927)

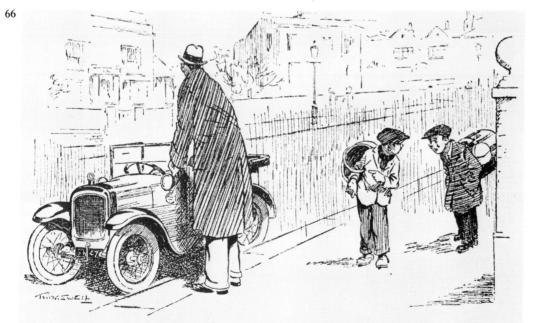

66

First Arrival (much impressed). "BLIMEY, GINGER, YOU AIN'T ARF MISSED SOMETHIN'! YOU OUGHT TO 'AVE SEEN 'IM UNCURL 'ISSELF."

67

68

Roller printed Cretonne manufactured by F. W. Grafton & Co.
/*Crown Copyright, Victoria and Albert Museum*

The motor car, as the disarming glass cruet demonstrates, even invaded the dining room. Not all dining rooms, of course, and the furniture from Gordon Russell Ltd suggests that eating at home could be a very congenial and civilised activity in which no extraneous novelties were necessary.

The 1927 cooker produced by the General Electric Company is a strange contemporary of the Baby Austin and the Russell furniture. Both of the latter, one for reasons of economy and the other out of a concern for elegance, achieved a lightness of form which the cooker stoutly rejects.

The motor car had shaken off any visible signs of its ancestry in the horse-drawn carriage, but the cooker still suggests the solid robustness of construction and reliability of performance which was so endearing a feature of the earlier coal ranges. Reliable it no doubt was, but its bulk and solidity seem both incongruous with the weightless and invisible power it employed and careless of the space which was becoming increasingly valuable in the shrinking kitchens for which it was intended.

CURTAINS 1927

1928

Whilst many families still lacked any reasonable home, the home building programme began to suffer an excess of success. Stanley Baldwin, speaking in Winchester, declared that 'it is no exaggeration to say that in fifty years, at the rate so-called improvements are being made, the destruction of all the beauty and charm with which our ancestors enhanced their towns and villages will be complete.'

The most sinister aspect of the desecration of the environment to which Baldwin referred was Ribbon Development. It was a simple process. Detached or semi-detached houses were built in two rows, of indefinite length, one either side of an existing or newly constructed road. Individual homes had a splendid view of the countryside from the back windows and the occupants seemed not to be dissuaded from the conviction that they were in an idyllic setting by the less pleasing view from the front windows. No more damaging an arrangement of houses can be imagined. The traveller was insulated from the countryside by the development, the development itself scarred and scratched the landscape with unwanted interruptions of a previously coherent pattern, the provision of services to the house was wasteful. Only the developments in transport facilities, both car and rail, made it a practical possibility.

The houses of which these ribbons were made were extraordinary in their superficial references to past styles of architecture. They were so inappropriate, so debased and flimsy in application as to become a vernacular statement of the time geared wholly to the owners' passion for individuality.

As builders became more adept at the pastiche the developments changed from strings of houses, each with the same inexplicable eccentricity, to rows in which each, by some nuance, differed from its neighbour. Interiors were generally identical.

'*The typical English home is undoubtedly the small country house where family life is provided for in a more ample manner than is possible in town. . . . . .;*

'*There has been some outcry in certain quarters for an architecture which shall represent the present, rather than copy another period . . . . But what we are inclined to forget is that the architecture of the homes of the 15th and 16th Centuries that have happily come down to us is much too good to part with. Our own age is rather one of wonderful inventions.*

'*The few houses which we see here and there which do strike a very original note are, unfortunately, not remarkable for beauty. What is still more serious, they are not conducive to the happy home life of the family.*

'*Nobody can be too thankful for the many blessings that . . . . . modern inventions have introduced to the home, but man cannot live on these things alone. When they are skillfully added to the old home, or to the new home built in the traditional manner, then, perhaps, we touch the nearest point to perfection which is possible.*

'*In an old house you may have to pass through one bedroom to get to another . . . . . People lived somewhat differently; today it would be intolerable and modification of the design is essential.*

'*Suitable provision has also to be made for several bathrooms which are now considered necessary; the house with a bathroom is out of date.*

'*The wide hearth with its firedogs and chimney corner seat . . . . . is an old tradition that can never die. It is the centre of the family life, and around its cheerful blazing logs the family circle will gather on the long winter evenings.*

'*We shall, of course, need central heating too, an even temperature over the whole house is desireable; but family life and true homeliness, to say nothing of hospitality, could not be maintained around a radiator!*'

from 'The Typical English Home' by the Marquis D'Oisy in *The Ideal Home* (June 1928)

71

Charlady of Ultra-Modern's studio (to privileged friend). "'E NOW 'AS AN EASEL BY 'IS BEDSIDE TO BE READY TO PAINT. 'E *FORGOT* 'IS LAST NIGHT-MARE."

A woman often enough accepted that her place was at all times in the home, evenings included. When the essentials of the day's work of housekeeping was done, out would come the knitting. Perhaps knitting was proof of the oft-repeated legend that 'woman's work is never done': or maybe the legend seemed undeniably true because of the knitting, but in many homes it made the difference between a Fair Isle jumper, a woolly hat and scarf, or nothing to keep out the winter cold.

By 1928 knitting was just one of a legion of crafts practised by the whole family. In 1920 Dryad Handicrafts had issued a one-page catalogue of materials for basket making. The 1928 edition (from which the drawings on page 53 are taken) ran to 150 pages. New sections were included to cover Poker Work, Soft Toy Making, Silverwork, Jewellery and Felt Work. The years between had seen the addition of instructions for crafts as diverse as Barbola, Batik, Bead-work, Lacemaking, Lacquer Work and Leatherwork, Papier Mache, Pottery and Pewter Work, Raffia and Rushwork, Rugmaking, Weaving, Water Colouring and Woodwork.

Not everybody approved of the cult of home-crafts (as may be read in the quotation from John Betjemen's article on page 63) but many could look back in later life to blissful evenings in front of a coal fire, wireless playing, when, armed with rug-hooks, the whole family worked away at a rug to enhance the scene the following year – by which time they might be trying their hands at embroidery, canework, or toy-carving. For most, a harmless and fascinating interest produced a few bits of bric-a-brac with family associations.

On the other hand, for Captain Vale, the creative impulse was geared to bigger things. He designed and built 'Corona-del-Mar' – a house which achieved notoriety in 1928 as the Wonder House of Rottingdean. The photograph (on the opposite page) could hardly be expected to do justice to the extraordinary juxtaposition of furnishings housed under the domed ceiling of this tremendous 'do-it-yourself' enter-prise.

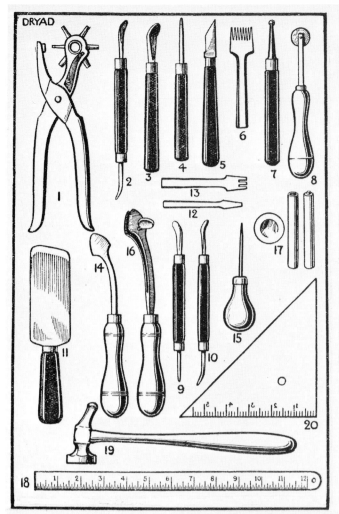

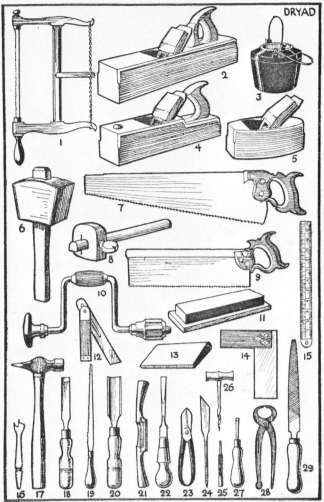

Roller printed cotton designed by Mea Augerer.
/Crown Copyright, Victoria and Albert Museum

Ladies who did not conform to the dictum that 'a woman's place is in the home' were the flappers – and 1928 was their year: the year in which the voting age for women was reduced from 35 to 21 years.

Here are two of those lovely girls, perhaps setting off to a thé-dansant, leaving a hall decorated in the absolutely most up-to-date style. 'New Art' was somewhat out-of-key with the staircase but that was of small consequence if one kept one's mind firmly on the importance of being right up to the minute.

Whilst the flesh-and-blood Flappers were out and about and, to their parents' consternation, 'burning the candle at both ends', the ideal young lady stood in homes without number, in effigy. Idealised young womanhood was a favourite subject for the statuettes which were almost essential to the well-appointed small home. Alsatian dogs, angel fish and elephants were high on the list of popular ornaments, but somehow their kind became stereotyped, whereas the girls appeared in amazing diversity, clothed, part-clothed and naked, of glass, ceramics or plaster; pure, pert or provocative. Occasionally, tortured into a crino-lined tea cosy, she was more than a pretty face and did something useful.

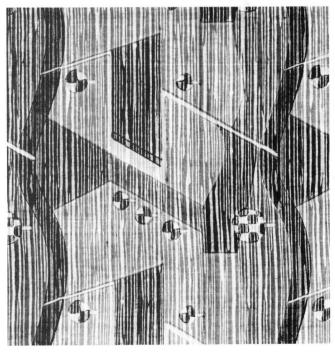

CURTAINS 1928

1929

Due south of Greenwich (The Meridian Monument defines the very line) on the Sussex coast is Peacehaven. It is perhaps unfair to pick on this particular development to illustrate the complement to Ribbon Development which most disfigured the English Countryside during the inter-war years. The name, which so clearly defines the aspirations of the settlers, the site, which was idyllic until the settlement occurred, and the manner of the development, which can be appreciated from the upper photograph – all conspire to make it a classic example of haphazard and sporadic home building in an area without an urban core, without places of work and, in the end, lacking the pleasures which promised before building began.

In 1929 almost any land in Britain was recognised as potential building land. If development was for some reason prohibited the owner could expect to be compensated for his loss of potential gain. Sometimes a small plot would be purchased and the house built upon it would disturb the pleasure of all but the occupants for miles around. (Affection can develop for any home, however ugly or misplaced; and once inside, it can't be seen anyway!). Sometimes the great estates of Country Houses and more often large tracts of open country were purchased and split into single building plots for development that was uncontrolled save for observance of building bye-laws.

A fearful visual indigestion resulted from the 'enlightened self-interest' of families who struggled to afford a home of their own, allied to the sometimes more ruthless self-interest of speculators who saw a way to private riches through an exploitation of undeveloped land.

The period was not one when idealists and conservationists could expect a very patient hearing. The case that house purchase would increase national stability and minimise class distinctions was much more appealing.

'If you are going to purchase a home, consider whether the district is one likely to expand with good-class property so as to increase the value of your investment.

'Look carefully at the planning of your home and garden, too. You will need to make the most of available space.

'Today, built-in furniture may help you. Remember that labour-saving in the home is not achieved just by the acquisition of a number of labour-saving mechanical devices, but begins with the planning of your home to help organisation and save waste of energy, time and thought in its daily round.

'How is the kitchen designed? What will your needs be for hot water, winter and summer – or for cooking – or, perhaps heating? What methods will suit you as economical in fuel for the heat you need – and yet be a workable proposition for the staff you intend to maintain?

'Is the kitchen planned conveniently for service to the dining-room? Think of your home in wet or cold weather, even if you purchase it in summer!

'Has your wife got all the provision she needs in kitchen and larder? are the lighting points in the places where they will give you adequate service?

'Don't rush into your acquisition of a new home. Look around and see what will be the best proposition for yourself and your family and then find out how best to use your available resources to the greatest advantage.

'The latest ideas in domestic architecture and town-planning can be seen by a tour of the estates which are being developed throughout the country . . . . .'

from 'Why live in town?' in *The Ideal Home* (June 1929)

80

THE SIMPLE NOTE IN MODERN DECORATION.

Ecstatic Female. "MY DEAR, HOW *EXQUISITELY* UNFURNISHED!"

Year after year the Ideal Home Exhibition drew families with established homes and young couples with no more than a glint in the eye to see what the World and his Wife should be doing about the house. Three pictures give the flavour of 1929.

Above, help for people struggling with the problems of a very small living room – an oak table which could be 'instantly' converted into a settee.

To the right, help for people undecided about the way they should furnish the best bedroom. Lots of ripping ideas in the top picture, but really, the elders would be saying, the room below is more like home.

82

83

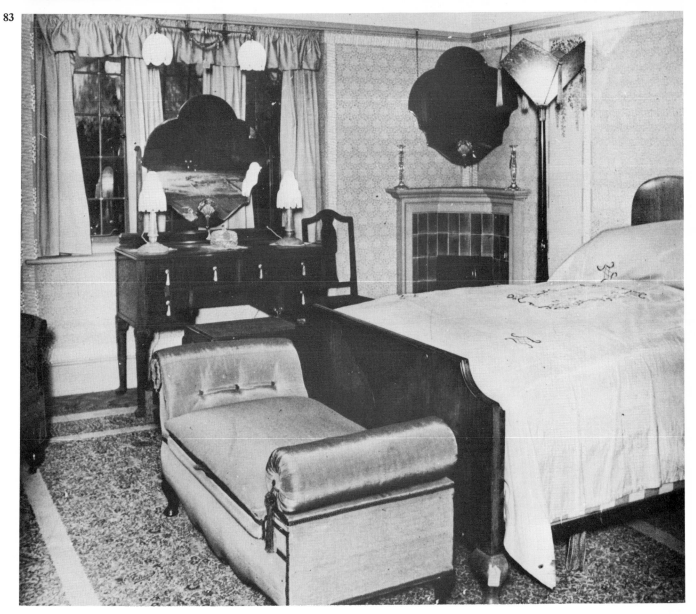

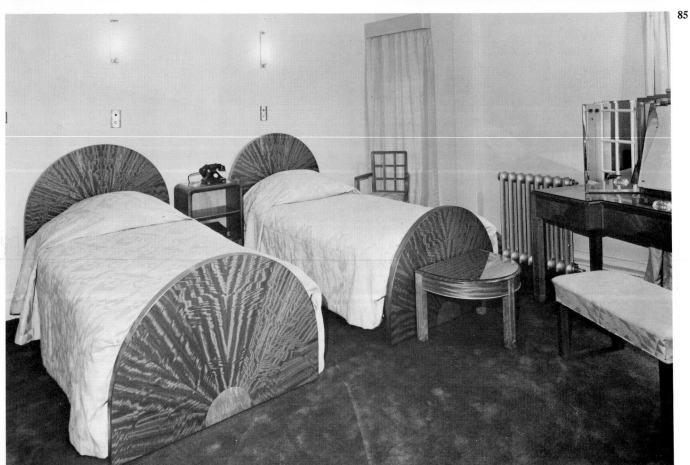

Roller printed cotton designed by Minnie McLeish.
/*Crown Copyright*, Victoria and Albert Museum

Whilst the Ideal Home Exhibition was careful to do honour to the dreams and the realities of domestic life for people of many persuasions the furniture makers and suppliers limited their concern to providing what they thought right for the people they served.

The bedroom furniture here is from two sources held in high regard by limited sections of society.

Gordon Russell's 1929 Coxwell Bedroom furniture, above, was made for his time and all time.

Opposite is a suite from Betty Joel Limited, made for **that** time, with lively imagination. Colonel and Mrs Joel felt the pulse of their contemporaries sensitively and responded with flair. The cloche hat is posed nicely on the dressing table and the sunburst motif (surely the symbol which signifies the inter-war years) makes a restrained appearance on the drawer fronts.

The third picture is a glimpse forward to Betty Joel in 1935. The sunburst is still about, boldly as to scale but only hinted at in detail by the ingenious use of contrasting timbers and the careful arrangement of veneers on the head and foot of the beds.

CURTAINS 1929

1930

3lb self raising flour	11d
2lb granulated sugar	6d
1lb cocoa	2s
1lb Indian tea	2s 8d
20 cigarettes	11½d
1 bottle whisky	12s 6d
1 pint pale ale	7d
3 tablets toilet soap	1s 6d
400 yard reel of cotton	5½d
1 yard scarlet flannel	3s 9d
10lb wedding cake	£1 10s

1930 marked the tenth anniversary of the founding of Welwyn Garden City. Whilst it was still incomplete, it is time to take a look, for it was at the other extreme from the reckless speculative building of, for example, Peacehaven.

The town is the second to have been built in England on the basis of Ebenezer Howard's ideas in *Tomorrow*, the book published in 1898 and re-published in 1902 as *Garden Cities of Tomorrow*. The Garden Cities and Town Planning Association definition is 'a town planned for industry and healthy living; of a size that makes possible a full measure of social life, but not larger; surrounded by a belt of rural land; the whole of the land being in public ownership or held in Trust for the community.'

Howard, a short-hand writer through most of his life, was knighted in 1927 and died in 1928. He had hit on an idea which was perfectly in accord with the English ideal of home: a development sufficiently controlled to allow sensible lay-out of streets and sufficiently standardised in design of homes to avoid random indiscretions – yet responding to the wish of many householders to express some clear individuality.

There were, of course, aspects of the idea which commentators found bizarre, not to say hilarious. For want of a better precedent, the medieval village green was seen as an acceptable form; disciples from the Arts and Crafts Movement joined with the Fabians and gave the concept artistic and social motives of mixed and esoteric appeal. In obedience to the dicta timber was felled amd milled and bricks made on site. This was rewarding material for the humorists. It smacked of sandals and vegetarianism; but the people in the homes were happily unconcerned.

'Woe to the backwardness of Arts and Crafts! Woe to the Revivals! Woe, too, to those young men in decorating firms who stipple the drawing rooms of South Audley Street and Kensington with old gold, midsummer green and dragon's blood red. Their end is near. It is useless to imagine that the best is hand done nowadays. We can make it in the factories much better. We only lack intelligent designers.

'The present day has been reached at last. Little can those persons called "cubists" (and we only hear about them now in the pages of Punch*) be aware of their profound influence over the unintelligent. Stained glass is giving up its old* Art Nouveau *roots and stems and sunsets; it is becoming all cone and oblong and parallelogram. Chintz curtains are being taken down from Kate Greenaway bedrooms and "bold, simple" stuff in orange and black or blue and yellow is being put up in their stead. This results in the "awf'lly modern" period of decoration, started in 1920 and known as "jazz". Cushions, whose colours resemble the allied flags, are strewn about the parlour; mother's old ornaments are swept off the mantelpiece and healthy daughters in simple frocks put handmade and badly constructed toys and quaintresses in their place. The pitchpine chairs and sideboards are painted blue and yellow. The lampshade is made at home. A million women set to on every "work" there is. With fingers busy at last, after long emancipation, they do "batik-work", "poker-work", "stencilling", "fretwork", "copperwork", "metalwork", "lampshade work" and any other work that can be devised. The harm they have done is terrific, for now the truly simple efforts of Le Corbusier and Dufy are hardly appreciated. They are merely regarded as "jazz" gone a little too far. But the work that the French, Germans and Swedes are doing speaks for itself when we bear in mind the axioms of Soane in that their simplicity is the result not of whim but of logic. Indeed, enrichment is not our strong point. "For it is in Simplicity that all real Decoration is to be found. A multitude of Ornament may materially injure, but never can improve, the effect of any composition. The great Beauty of Architectural Composition consists more in a due regard to Proportion, Symmetry and Propriety of Form, both general and detailed, and in apposite decoration, than in a great Profusion of enrichments" (Soane; Lecture XI).*

'It is too late to mend what has been done already. Villadom is too fragile to stand repair, but we can leave off our revivals and our bad workmanship so that the flowers which we put on our tables do not stand, as they do now, a mute excuse for the badness of the furniture.'

from A Guide to the Recent History of Interior Decoration in the *Architectural Review* of May 1930, by John Betjeman who in 1977 didn't 'wholly agree with the happy arrogance which gave birth to that article'.

89

RECESS
CUPBOARD.

WILL'S CIGARETTES.

WILLS'S CIGARETTES
Nº 24
HOUSEHOLD HINTS
2ND SERIES OF 50.

The Uses of a Lemon.

Five useful hints: (1) Slices of lemon rubbed over the forehead will sometimes relieve a headache. (2) Lemon juice and glycerine rubbed overnight into the skin greatly improves its appearance. (3) One or two drops of lemon juice will keep mosquitoes away. (4) Many people prefer a cup of tea served in the Russian style, with a thin slice of lemon taking the place of milk, sugar being added to taste. (5) Lemons keep fresh for several weeks in a bowl of cold water, which should be changed frequently. They also keep well when packed in dry silver sand.

W. D. & H. O. WILLS

ISSUED BY THE IMPERIAL TOBACCO CO.
(OF GREAT BRITAIN & IRELAND) LTD.

WILLS'S
CIGARETTES.

PAPERHANGING.

WILLS'S CIGARETTES
Nº 33
HOUSEHOLD HINTS
2ND SERIES OF 50.

How to make a Pouffe.

Use a good quality cretonne, printed linen, tapestry or velvet; poor material is not worth the trouble of making up. Having decided the size required (18 in. diameter, by 12 or 15 in. high is a convenient size), proceed to cut circular pieces for top and bottom. Tack material flat on a board and use a cardboard disc as pattern; if these circles are not true, the finished pouffe will not be symmetrical. Carefully seam top and bottom pieces to border piece, leaving ends of latter open for insertion of filling. *This must be packed evenly and very tightly*, otherwise the pouffe will not retain its shape. Stitch up material, press pouffe into shape and finish with cord as illustrated.

W. D. & H. O. WILLS

ISSUED BY THE IMPERIAL TOBACCO CO.
(OF GREAT BRITAIN & IRELAND) LTD.

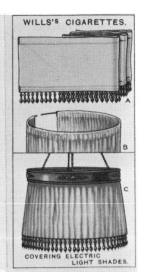

WILLS'S CIGARETTES.

A

B

C

COVERING ELECTRIC
LIGHT SHADES.

WILLS'S CIGARETTES
Nº 12
HOUSEHOLD HINTS
2ND SERIES OF 50.

Recess Cupboard.

Dwellers in flats, and others who desire to make the most of limited space, may welcome this suggestion for utilizing a recess in a living or bed-sitting room. The upper portion of the cupboard is separately curtained and fitted for stores. On the left the lower part is fitted with sliding drawers for clothes, etc., and a rail for shoes below. On the right is a cupboard for hanging coats, etc. This space-saving fitment could be cheaply and easily constructed by a handyman.

W. D. & H. O. WILLS

ISSUED BY THE IMPERIAL TOBACCO CO.
(OF GREAT BRITAIN & IRELAND) LTD.

WILLS'S CIGARETTES.

THE USES OF A LEMON.

WILLS'S CIGARETTES
30
HOUSEHOLD
HINTS
A SERIES OF 50.

Paperhanging.

In good class work the joints are *butted*, both edges of paper being trimmed close. In *lap-joining*, only one margin is removed. Having prepared walls and cut lengths of paper required, decide on order in which walls are to be papered. It is customary to begin at a window or an angle of wall, and arrange so that overlaps face strongest light. Having pasted first length, and folded over ends, ascend the ladder and holding paper an inch or so from the top, allow it to unwind and press lightly into position at top. Test with plumb-line and smooth from centre outwards with clean brush or duster. Crease top and bottom edges with scissors, and trim neatly.

ISSUED BY THE IMPERIAL TOBACCO CO.
(OF GREAT BRITAIN & IRELAND) LTD.

WILLS'S CIGARETTES.

A

B

C

HOW TO MAKE A POUFFE.

WILLS'S CIGARETTES
Nº 42
HOUSEHOLD HINTS
2ND SERIES OF 50.

Covering Electric Light Shades.

The renewal of old and faded silk shades is quite a simple matter. In the type of fitting illustrated (c) the shade is carried on a circular frame of wire fixed by screws to the inner side of the decorated copper band. Unscrew and detach the old shade, and using the old silk as a pattern, cut the new piece to the same size and stitch up as shown, A. A bead trimming of suitable colour, though not essential, provides a handsome finish and makes the shade hang better. When dark-coloured silk is used, better reflection is secured by inserting an inner shade of white or cream silk on a *slightly smaller* frame.

W. D. & H. O. WILLS

ISSUED BY THE IMPERIAL TOBACCO CO.
(OF GREAT BRITAIN & IRELAND) LTD.

ASH TRAYS, MATCH STANDS, TOBACCO JARS, ETC.

B.G. 6068
HEAVY GLASS TRAY
With Electro-plated Match Holder and
Cigar or Cigarette Rests.
Size 4½ in. diameter .. each   7/6

B.G. 1
NESTS OF ASH TRAYS
Nickel-plated coloured.
Ash Trays, with Rests and Stands
complete.
Nest of 4 Trays, 9/9 and 11/- complete.
Nest of 6 Trays, "A" quality, 16/9
each complete.

B.G. 6073
**HALL-MARKED PLAIN SILVER
MATCH HOLDER**
With Ash Tray and two Cigar or
Cigarette Rests.
Size 4 in. diameter .. each   36/-

B.G. 7057
ASH BOWL
**MANUFACTURED BY THE
SOCIETY**
For use with or without water.

		Large size.	Small size.
Polished Brass	each	5/3	3/9
„ Copper	„	5/3	3/9
Nickel-plated	„	7/-	4/6

B.G. 6067
**HEAVY COPPER YACHT
ASH BOWL**
**MANUFACTURED BY THE
SOCIETY**
With cork for knocking ash from pipe.

Size 4 in. diameter	..	each	11/-
„ 4½ „	..	„	12/6
„ 5 „	..	„	13/6
„ 5½ „	..	„	14/9
„ 6 „	..	„	15/6

Also similar Wood "KNOCK
KNOBBY" Ash Bowl, 6 in. diameter
Each 7/6
And others .. .. .. each 5/6

B.G. 7128
HALL-MARKED SILVER TRAY
With Glass Match Holder mounted with
Silver Cup and Rim.
Size, diameter of tray, 3¼ in. each 21/-

B.G. 6095
**AIRTIGHT EARTHENWARE
TOBACCO JAR**
With Brass Triangle.
Size to hold 4 oz. tobacco each   8/-
„ „ 12 „ „ 9/3

B.G. 6061
SILVER-PLATED ASH TRAY
Size 4¾ in. diameter .. each   4/6

B.G. 7137
**HANDSOME DOULTON WARE
TOBACCO JAR**
Airtight, with patent plated spring fastener.
Size to hold 12 oz. tobacco .. .. each 14/3
Toby Pattern Jar, spring top .. .. „ 12/-

B.G. 7052
WOOD PIPE RACK
MANUFACTURED BY THE SOCIETY
To hold 7 pipes.

Oak, stained light or dark	..	.. each	15/-
Oak, dark stained, to hold 4 pipes	..	„	11/3
Also in Brass	.. ..	„	42/-

B.G. 7061
HEAVY COPPER TOBACCO JAR
MANUFACTURED BY THE SOCIETY
Tinned inside.
Size outside, 5½ × 3½ in .. .. .. each 31/6
„ „ 4½ × 3½ „ .. .. .. „ 25/-

ALL PRICES ARE SUBJECT TO MARKET FLUCTUATIONS

What, it is fair to ask, has W. F. Eames picture 'When did you last see your Father' to do with an ordinary English home of the thirties? It is to do with smoking.

There were few misgivings about tobacco during the inter-war years. It had been Father's comfort in the wartime trenches and, after the war, many Mothers took up the habit. The card that came with each packet of cigarettes was passed to the children, so all the family shared in the fun.

The cards covered a tremendous range of interest, from ballroom dancing to naval battles. The home came in for its share of attention. If Father decided to make a fitted wardrobe or Mother a jolly bedspread the children lost the swops needed to make up the complete set of 'Household Hints' or to join the skimming during school break (cards were flicked from a start line towards a wall; nearest to the wall at the end of a game took all).

As time went by the threat of a card famine grew worse. One maker produced squares of silk, in place of cards, printed with Flowers, Birds or Flags of All Nations. Even if these weren't made up into cushion covers they were no use for skimming! Worst of all came the card gift-offers: 48 cards together made up some popular picture and a complete set could be exchanged for a print suitable for home decoration. That meant no cards, or even silk squares, for the children. One of those pictures was 'When did you last see your Father' and it was to be seen in the sitting room of many an ordinary English home.

The 1930 Ideal Home Show included an exhibit of 'A predicted Modern Nursery'. It can be safely assumed that it was an eye-catcher rather than a serious suggestion. It is unlikely that anybody thought future babies were to be confronted by Mother or Nanny in tin hat and gauntlets.

Many small children were still enjoying traditional wooden toys; others were moving on to newer things. Constructional toys and games grew in number and complexity – there were Meccano, Mobacco and Lotts bricks for example, the last capable even of being put together with 'real mortar'. Toy soldiers, farm and zoo animals of moulded and painted lead and toy trains of folded metal sheet were still going strong. Model trains were in a different class altogether, often acquired over a long period by family subscription; quite frequently the interest continued into retirement long after Son was a Father himself.

Come November it was 'Penny for the Guy Mister', a five

shilling box of fireworks lovingly handled until nearly all the gunpowder had fallen out and, on the Fifth, sparklers and bengal lights, bonfire and chestnuts, supper and bed.

Come Christmas, it was an 18in Hercules bicycle if you were twelve, a pair of roller skates, a knitting Nancy or one of the newest family table games to play on Boxing Day. The Christmas tree was anything from a real pine tree scraping the ceiling to a mere 18in folding, stiff-branched wire framework for green shredded paper 'needles' (each rigid little arm tipped with a shiny red blob) standing unsteadily, geometric and unpromising, in a red wooden pot. Whichever it was the magic grew as it was decorated with glass balls, tinsel and electric fairy lights. Unlike the wax candles, which would totter so dangerously in the spring-clip tin holders, the 'fairy lights' could be left shining all evening.

'Loopy'. Block printed cotton by Enid Marx.
|*Bath Crafts Study Centre Collection*

Although Jazz Modern had knocked on the Nursery door it had made no impression on Toyland. Elsewhere around the house the impact was stronger. It might be too risky to go in for a complete re-furnishing scheme, but if it was time to buy a new tea-set the choice was there. The three examples here were all in use around 1930. That at the top left is a tea service designed by painter Frank Brangwyn and made by Doulton. Below it and at the other end of the design spectrum is the Jazz Modern contribution from Shelley Potteries. Above is the in-between, combining free flowing printed and hand-painted decoration on strongly geometric and angular forms produced by Paragon China.

CURTAINS 1930

Between 1921 and 1931 about 1.6 million dwellings were constructed. Over 2.3 million more would be completed by the end of the 1930s, mostly in suburbia.

Between the muddle of Peacehaven and the rectitude of Welwyn Garden City was a disconcerting variety of suburbs. Some were uncontrolled conglomerations; others were garden suburbs exhibiting the physical charcteristics which Ebenezer Howard condoned. In some, every house differed; in others, all were the same. The upper picture of Orpington and the lower of Esher suggest substantial differences in the incomes of the householders, but both typify the products of the building boom which started about 1931 and continued through the decade.

Suburbanites cannot be typed any more than urban or rural inhabitants, but they were normally white-collar workers and occasionally artisans. Social relationships were often strong between neighbours and it was suggested that there was more frequent isolation in urban areas and that more powerful family links were retained in old established villages.

The majority of houses were semi-detached, with three bedrooms, two living rooms, bathroom, kitchen and a garage or space for a garage in a small garden. A one-family house was well suited to a married couple with two children, but was often pressed into housing a widowed parent in addition.

The aesthetic of the suburbs was the despair of intellectuals and highbrows generally. It was, indeed, a mess. Building to a price after a hundred years of revivals of one architectural style and another was more than most architects, let alone builders, could manage. The evocative embellishments became ever more frenzied and flimsy. Most occupants, many owning a home for the first time, thought the houses very artistic. They didn't feel at all like the Dreadful Little Man in *Punch* who didn't go with anything.

'We find people beginning to reckon up ways in which they can take their pleasures within the range of the home circle at the least possible expense.

'There are many forms which these pleasures can take . . . . . books . . . . . the cultivation of gardens . . . . . the arts of cookery and housewifery, which have been in sad decline during the past century of urbanisation . . . . .

'In addition to the re-emergence of features which used to sweeten old-time home life, we are fortunate in the influence which modern scientific invention is exercising in making the home a place where amusement, education and news can all be obtained within its walls as readily as elsewhere. The social philosopher of the future will be able to write much about the revolution which is being accomplished in our generation by the gramophone and the wireless, in banishing dullness and introducing back to the home the content which comes from variety of interest. Nor should it be long, we surmise, before, through television and the home cinema, it will become possible for the average man and woman to find full satisfaction for the eye as well as the ear in the field of recreation and entertainment, without wasting time and energy on restless movement in trains, 'buses and motor-cars. These joys cannot at present, perhaps, be equally shared by town and country; but it does not take a very far-seeing intelligence to perceive that modern urban civilisation has run almost the full course of its growth, and that a movement of decentralisation and de-urbanisation is now under weigh, which will bring back a much larger proportion of our people to contact with the land and the country in some form or other. We may feel sure, therefore, that the home, like the village, is emerging at last from its long eclipse, and is about to recover its full effectiveness as a stabilising, but not static, social institution'.

leader in *The Listener* (1931)

101

Hostess (at reception of Moderns). "WHAT ON EARTH MADE YOU ASK THAT DREADFUL LITTLE MAN? HE SIMPLY DOESN'T GO WITH ANYTHING."

Roller printed cotton manufactured for Liberty and Co.
/*Crown Copyright, Victoria and Albert Museum*

In spite of the growth and popularity of the suburbs railway carriage homes, which so upset Max Beerbohm in 1920, were still preferred by determined individualists.

When Max made his complaint it seems that no one had need for ambitious extensions, improvements or for that matter – camouflage and Mr Rymer, many years later, was still of that mind. He and Queen Victoria both made use of this carriage; the Queen used it to carry her person, Mr Rymer used it as a seaside bungalow.

Mr Marston Manthorpe, a railwayman who began his career as a Lad-Porter and ended it as Station Master at County School Station, Norfolk was more advanced. On his retirement he realised his ambition to build a house 'of his own design' – two railway carriages with a lean-to extension of brick (conservatory and smoking saloon?). Clearly a restrained man, he showed sensitive consideration for the railway vernacular in the embellishment and cladding of the extension; here he is in 1931 digging his garden, the building work complete.

The last picture reveals what the really ambitious brothers R. and G. Horton could do. Here they show off their thatched carriage home to visitors, who share for a moment the rural delights.

CURTAINS 1931

1932

The Town and Country Planning Act of 1932 defined a statuary concern with the qualities of the existing environment. Designed to ensure that land be considered as permanent open space until a proper case was made for its development, it offered aid to local authorities who wanted to set up satellite towns and obliged them to prepare town planning schemes.

In the event, the Act was less effective than its sponsors and supporters had hoped. The establishment of satellite towns was long delayed. The urge to build overcame the merits of restraint and by proposing 'zoning' of houses at 1, 8 or 12 to the acre it intensified the tendency for families to be segregated by income difference.

The wisdom of the Garden City Idea was accepted by the Act, but town planner Thomas Sharpe, whilst condoning the concept of building a series of towns of limited size, found it ' . . . grotesque that modern towns should be dominated by a back-to-the-land movement of thirty years ago and a modern town-dweller should not be allowed to build or obtain a house unless it has a small-holding attached to it.'

He was not alone in his anger at the spread and sprawl around major cities, but his conviction that the countryside could only be saved by making towns as compact as the minimum requirements of public health would allow, and that towns could be made pleasurable only by limiting rurality to the country, was too sophisticated a concept for people who had inherited towns long since deprived of their civic dignity.

The influence of the Act, of Garden Cities and of Thomas Sharpe had not inhibited the resourceful independence of Mr T. Martin, who built his own house of concrete blocks, just the way, it seems, that Mrs Martin wanted it, in Hookwood, Horsley, Surrey. The same goes for Mr Chapman, who built 'Upatree' in one month for £100. By 1933, when the photograph was taken, 'visitors from all parts of the World' had been to see it.

'One has to admit that at the present time in 1932 the taste of the antique is the favourite flavour of eighty per cent of the population, or at least is supposed to be by the builder and furniture makers. What is the alleged ideal home offered to the dwellers in Metroland? A gabled house with bogus beams and lattice windows. And Mr. Drage's idea of what the city man likes to come back to in the evenings? A sham ingle nook and a gas log fire. With what sort of curtains and rugs does the city man's wife brighten up the drawing-room? Old English chintzes and Persian carpets. What is that his mother-in-law is irritably working on her tambour? A tea-cosy of Jacobean design. And so it goes on.

'Fortunately there are signs that, although the public continues to be fed with "antique", it is beginning to feel a little sick. But equally, unfortunately, it is offered an unwholesome alternative. I have already stated my conviction that the most formidable obstacle to the new movement is commercial modernism. Someone in an unhappy moment invented the word "Modernistic", a repellent title but uncannily expressive of the particular blasphemy it represents. Just as at an earlier date persons and things were referred to as "so artistic", now they are described as "quite modernistic", and in each case one knows only too well what to expect. The modernistic craze is kept lively by the same stimuli as the antique vogue-snobbery and delusion. Manufacturers and shopkeepers persuade innocent people that it is smart and even a little daring to possess what they call "modernistic" furniture and their customers delude themselves into thinking they have superior minds which can "understand" modern art. None of them know quite what they are talking about but the customers feel flattered and the tradesmen find it pays to be modernistic. Actually modernistic design is entirely meaningless and the product of a venal commercialism. Manufacturers and dealers, snuffing the prevailing wind, call up their hack designers and command them to "jazz things up a bit". At first the designers are bewildered but a little peeping and eavesdropping gives them a hint of "what the old man is talking about' and very soon they "get the hang of the thing", after that it is only a matter of time before another North Kensington drawing-room "goes modernistic".

'This is the second impediment of taste, the last and worst being a dreadful blending of two fallacies, a fatal mariage de convenance between modernist and antique – the jazz rep cushion in the sham Jacobean chair, the "abstract" rug from the Tottenham Court Road dozing by the brick hearth . . . .

'What is so vitally needed to-day is a sane grasp of the character of the modern expression. Names, labels and catchwords are quickly learnt but what they stand for is only vaguely understood. Half of us do not realize that we are living in a revolution which is gradually changing the form of every familiar object. We must learn the purpose of this change and the logic of its evolution'.

from *Room and Book* by Paul Nash (The Soncino Press Ltd 1932)

107

House-Agent. "A MOST DESIRABLE MAISONETTE, SIR."
Client. "AH! AND I SEE IT'S ALSO GOT A GARDENETTE AND A GARAGETTE."

'Shall we stay in and listen to the wireless or go to the pictures?' was a common question in the 1932 home.

The number of Radio Receiving Licences supporting the BBC had passed the five million mark. The British Broadcasting Corporation, as it had become in 1926, celebrated its tenth anniversary by moving its London Studios from Savoy Hill to a new and lavish Broadcasting House near Oxford Circus. The receiver industry's faith had been rewarded. Homemade sets were no longer popular and it was estimated that £5 millions worth of business would result from the year's Radio Show at Olympia.

Ekco's SH25 broke new ground for the plastics industry by being contained in 'a modern richly figured Bakelite Cabinet of warm walnut shade'. It cost 15 guineas. The more splendid RG23 three-stage, all-electric radiogram was 'housed in a walnut cabinet richly figured and beautifully polished by a new process that produces a satin-like finish'.

Radio had arrived, and so had the talkies. They first came to the British Screen in 1929, but early applause for technical achievement gave way to criticism of poor quality. By 1932 the new problems of sound were overcome and the industry entered its Golden Era.

The Cinema, luxurious, warm and dark became an escape from dreary home surroundings and a stimulus to home improvement. In 1932 alone one could identify with Greta Garbo in the *Grand Hotel* and the home of *Mata Hari* (the bedroom alone had enough contrasting ideas for a terrace of houses). On a more pedestrian level the English film *Here's George* demonstrated, as can be seen opposite, the conveniences – and confusions – of an automated service flat.

The movie mags extended the interest beyond the screen. The *Film Lovers Annual* for the year gave a detailed and illustrated account of Marie Dressler's Beverly Hills Home ('its solid, red brick walls stand on a palm-shaded corner among the many Spanish and Moorish homes typical of this section'). In another article stars' favourite rooms are described in sufficient detail to allow of passable pastiche. It all encouraged a longing for more glamorous homes.

108

109

112

113

114

Screen printed satin cotton designed by Duncan Grant.
/*Crown Copyright, Victoria and Albert Museum*

Whilst from grim necessity a slum-dweller in the 1930s was compelled to make a home as best he could in the single, all-purpose room seen at top left, the dual-purpose room was receiving more premeditated attention elsewhere

The picture above is of a room in a house on the Bournville Estate and combines the functions of kitchen, scullery and dining room for the use of the whole family. Offering a minimum of space with basic and not the most up-to-date equipment – a solid-fuel range, a gas-fired laundry boiler and a glazed earthenware sink with wooden draining board, it nevertheless exudes a happiness denied to the urban slums.

Similar functions are combined at a more affluent level in two rooms at the Ideal Home Show. Spacious, admirably direct in design and layout, the kitchen dining room is generously well-equipped with a large two-oven gas cooking range, built-in sink with mixer tap, work bench and fitted cupboards. The dining facilities would no longer be intended for the use of resident servants, but for informal family meals. Not to be found in the average 'semi'.

The other room, a Bedroom-Boudoir, demonstrates a different taste and life-style and reveals an awkward design-eclecticism which was doubtless wholly acceptable to and greatly admired by many a 1932 observer.

CURTAINS 1932

1933

3lb self raising flour — 8½d
2lb granulated sugar — 4½d
1lb cocoa — 1s 9d
1lb Indian tea — 2s 6d
20 cigarettes — 11½d
1 bottle whisky — 12s 6d
1 pint pale ale — 7d
3 tablets toilet soap — 1s 6d
400 yard reel of cotton — 4½d
1 yard scarlet flannel — 3s
10lb wedding cake — £1 10s

The many 'for sale' or 'to let' signs apparent in 1933 resulted not so much from a glut of houses as a shortage of cash. The Government felt it necessary to confine expenditure on housing to the growing problem of slums.

An Act of Parliament cancelled housing subsidies except for slum clearance. The Minister of Health appealed for speedy action. The LCC planned to rehouse a quarter of a million people in ten years at a cost of £35 millions.

In June the *Architects Journal* published a number of cases to illustrate the seriousness of the problem: In Manchester – man, wife and six children in one room: in Liverpool – four families in one house, father, mother and six children in two upstairs rooms, one of which leaked, rent 7s 6d; in Sheffield – a parlour let at 6s to a man and wife with five children under ten, two of whom slept out. It was clearly a hard problem and Sir E. D. Simon, who wrote *The Anti Slum Campaign*, felt it was difficult to agree its full extent. He commented on the evidence of Manchester's Medical Officer of Health that 30,000 homes were unfit for human habitation. 'If we call these the slums of Manchester', he extrapolated, 'then the corresponding number of houses in England and Wales would probably be about 1,000,000. But there are in Manchester no less than 80,000 houses of similar type, all of which must be replaced before we are in sight of our goal. If we extend the word "slum" to cover these houses there are probably four million which come into that category and which are certainly a long way below any standard acceptable to public opinion today.'

By the end of the year, as though to symbolise the nation's concern, plans were completed to burn down the 100year-old Romany settlement on Hurtwood Hill and rehouse the gipsies in three-roomed corrugated iron bungalows at Walton-on-Thames. We don't know how the gipsies reacted.

'*The years have brought their changes. Water closets have superseded the earth and tin privies, though not so very long ago; the holes in the tiny back-yard walls from which the pestiferous tins were drawn when to be emptied of the ordure are still to be traced, the newer bricks contrasting in colour with those of the original wall. Fever is rarer: large families are no longer permitted to live in cellars; instead, by force of circumstance and in the simplicity of their natures, they pay much more than their grandparents did for the convenience of living in a single room over a cellar.*

'*The identical houses of yesterday remain, still valuable in the estate market even though the cost of their building has been paid for over and over again by successive tenants. The houses remain: streets of them where the blue-grey smoke swirls down like companies of ghosts from a million squat chimneys: jungles of tiny houses cramped and huddled together, the cradles of generations of the future. Places where men and women are born, live, love and die and pay preposterous rents for the privilege of calling the grimy houses 'home' . . . .*

'*That dirty hovel, home? Where else? In all the wide world, of all the sweet dreams and fond imaginings of such homes as were writ of or projected at the pictures, of them all, hers was that in North Street. None else. The rest were words in a book, shadows flickering on a screen. Dreams. If she went elsewhere and asked for admittance the people would say: "You don't live here. We don't know who you are" . . . . Dully, insistently, crushing came the realisation that there was no escape, save in dreams. All was a tangle; reality was too hideous to look upon: it could not be shrouded or titivated for long by the reading of cheap novelettes or the spectacle of films of spacious lives. They were only opiates and left a keener edge on hunger, made more loathsome reality's sores.*

'*When you went to the public baths and stood, after a days work, in a queue waiting your turn until the attendant beckoned you to a cubicle where was a bath half-filled with dirty water left by the girl or woman just quitted the place – you couldn't by any stretch of imagination, even when the attendant had drained off the water and washed the muck away, see it as anything other than what it was, Hanky Park, the small corner of the wide, wide world where you lived.*'

from *Love on the Dole* by Walter Greenwood (Jonathan Cape 1933) by permission of the Walter Greenwood Estate.

118

AFTER THE GALE.
"AND WHAT ABOUT THIS 'ERE 'ARF TIMBERIN? SHALL I PEEL ORF WHAT'S STUCK ON, OR SHALL I TACK UP WHAT'S BLOWED ORF?"

119

120

121

122

123

124

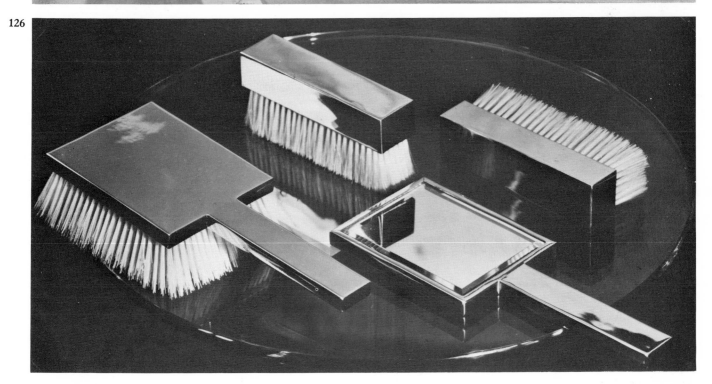

Not only the lovers on the dole in Hanky Park lived in homes without bathrooms. Heals still found it worthwhile to keep a stock of ewer and bowl toilet sets for people who needed them and were rich enough to equip their homes from the splendid London store.

The toilet set catalogue for 1933, whilst it illustrates a wide range of designs, six of which are shown here, gives no evidence of modern or Modernistic style. It must be the only area of pottery manufacture to be so deprived. But how sensible. It was a waning market and a modern home would have no need of such equipment.

Other products related to personal hygiene and appear-

ance suffered no such inhibition. Bathroom or no, making one's toilet was an increasingly important activity. The manufacturers of cosmetics and 'toiletries' were in a growing market. Young girls could hardly wait for the age when they could make-up respectably, old men would not shrink from dying their hair (but secretly, you understand); Mum, even, would use rouge and lipstick and Father did not bother to hide his brilliantine, bay rum and lavender water.

If there were facilities for bathing in the house this new concern certainly slowed up the process.

Screen printed cotton designed by Christopher Heal.
/*Heal and Son Limited, London*

The photograph of a bathroom, above, isn't true even though it's in a real house. Where are the sponge, the loofah, the pumice stone, soap, flannel, nail brush and where is the clutter of bottles, boxes and bibelots that the family seemed to cram onto the window sill? Still, it's real enough to show what any home purchaser would hope to see as a minimum in a newly-built house.

The room on the left is in another category. It's a bathroom that some might dream of but that Tilly Losch owned in her London home at 35 Wimpole Street. Designed by Paul Nash, it seems to have everything a 1933 bathroom could have: glazed walls, black equipment, tube lighting, a mirrored ceiling. Two of the features would not have appeared even a few years earlier. Tube lighting, though used in advertising as early as 1910, was seldom used domestically. Decorative glazed walls became a possibility only as new glass products flooded onto the market.

The vogue for glass resulted in some lamentable errors of decorative judgement but Paul Nash, with the rare sensibility to be expected of a brilliant artist, avoids the pitfalls and amply justifies the use of the material.

It is a very assured creation – and, what's more, there are two nice bottles on the window sill.

CURTAINS 1933

1934

For 8.6% of the insured workers who were unemployed in London in 1934, 44.2% in Gateshead and a staggering 67.8% without work in Jarrow, it was a cheerless year. For those with jobs there was never a better time to look for a home. It was a buyers' market. The cost of a three-bedroomed house with living room, scullery and bathroom was in some cases under £300, compared with £900 in 1920, about £400 in 1927 and £375 in 1939.

There were many efforts to tempt the family, which, if it didn't have the price of a house, had the mere 10% needed for a mortgage after the 1933 Housing Act had received Royal Assent. At Gidea Park in the Modern Homes Exhibition of 1934 eight houses were built to show the kaleidoscope of delights awaiting the people with more money. They were a strange assemblage. The lower picture shows one of them, a detached house designed by architects Skinner and Tecton which was a handsome statement of the new design principles presaged by Newways in 1926; but the other house above, symmetrical, with a pitched tiled roof, designed by architect John Leech, was perhaps more to the general taste.

'It is a very trying, and sometimes despairing task for the housewife to keep her family well-fed on the amount allowed her on the Labour Exchange; but if she is a good manager, it can be done, and all the little weekly accounts kept paid up-to-date.

'Take for example, the family of five, ie husband, wife, and three children. Their allowances will be 15s 3d the man, 8s his wife, and 2s each child, thus amounting to £1 9s 3d per week. The scale drawn up at the end gives an idea how best to lay out the money, for the most necessary items.

'We are very thankful to get the Dole, and every wife should do her best to make it go as far as possible, and not waste what other poor folks may be glad to have.

Expenses		List of Groceries for 6s 3d			
				tin syrup	5d
Rent	10s 0d	½ lb tea	5d	1 lb prunes	6d
Insurance	1s 0d	2 lb sugar	5d	pkt custard	1½d
Doctors' Club	1s 0d	½ lb butter	4½d		
Wood & Coal	1s 4½d	1 lb margarine	4d	4 matches	3d
Gas	2s 4d	3 tins condensed milk	9d	3 cooking eggs	4d
Bread	2s 4d	½ lb rice	2d	bar soap	4d
Vegetables	1s 6d	½ lb tapioca	2d	1 lb soda	1d
Groceries	6s 3d	3 lb flour	4½d	1 candle	½d
Milk	9d	pkt suet	4d	2 oxo cubes	2d
Meat	2s 6d	1 lb currants	6d	1 symingtons soup	2d
	£1 9 0½				6s 3d

Balance 2½d

A. B.'

From a note written by the wife of an unemployed man and printed in the *New Statesman and Nation* (31 March 1934) without any alteration or corrections.

131

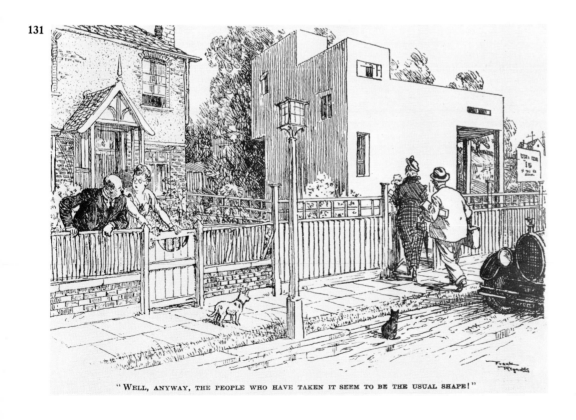

"WELL, ANYWAY, THE PEOPLE WHO HAVE TAKEN IT SEEM TO BE THE USUAL SHAPE!"

CALLOWBROOK ESTATE.
THE HEALTHIEST SPOT SOUTH OF BHAM

TO LET MODERN HOUSES TO LET

HALL
2 REC.
KITCHEN
GOOD SHOPPING

GARAGE
SPACE

3 BEDROOMS
BATHROOM *FITTED*
BASIN H AND C
MODERN SCHOOLS

ONLY 20 MINUTES CENTRE OF CITY

Warp printed Cretonne.
|Crown Copyright, Victoria and Albert Museum

Not all houses built in 1934 were as sound, lively and appealing as those built at Gidea Park. Nevertheless houses were available as thousands of notices testified. Some of them, alas, promoted unscrupulous and incompetent work.

Mrs Borders saw a sign in West Wickham. She bought a house for the then handsome sum of £693 with the help of a Building Society, who assured her it was properly built. She is pictured sitting in the porch, some time after the purchase, when wallpaper had detached itself, cracks had appeared, water had penetrated, floor boards had shrunk and beetles were inhabiting the joinery.

Mrs Borders stopped her mortgage payment. The Building Society sued for repossession. She counterclaimed for return of her money plus £1,000 for repairs, arguing that the Society had misrepresented the condition of the house and, the builder having gone into liquidation, lent money on inadequate security.

It was a famous case which did not end until the House of Lords exonerated the Building Society in 1941. Mrs Borders, the 'Tenants KC', lost but in the process inspired the creation of a number of Tenants Defence Leagues and became the heroine of thousands of disgruntled freeholders and tenants who felt they had been wickedly treated by the deplorable 'Jerry-builders'.

CURTAINS 1934

1935

1935 was the year of the Silver Jubilee of the reign of King George V and Queen Mary and was marked in many ways. Streets were decorated with garlands and flags, bonfires lit all around the coast, mugs made, medals struck.

The organisers of the year's Ideal Home Show, wishing to play their part in the jubilations, promoted the construction of the 'Jubilee Village' within the exhibition and the homes erected faithfully reflected the tastes of potential house-buyers. One of the homes is shown in the photograph above. Next door to it was a substantial essay in the fusion of modern living with Tudor symbols: half timbering, a long sweep of tiled roof extending downwards to cover the porch, leaded lights and a rather uncomfortable juxtaposition of ground floor bay with an oriel window above. Nevertheless, a good example of its kind.

The house in the foreground is of a different breed. It is difficult to detect any direct lineage from the past. There are elements such as the horizontal glazing panes in metal window frames, which are very much of their own time. The placing of the door on the corner of the block with a curved wall above is not a device familiar from previous house building. The complexity of the roof – something surely more easily avoided than resolved – and the combination of brick and stucco-rendered walls hints at a stronger concern with fantasy than with logic. This house is not a period pastiche but a modern romance – a series of picturesque falsehoods, an exercise of sympathetic imagination.

The confusion of form which allowed endless slight variations to distinguish one house from another was a reassuring rather than challenging mode for the potential owner. It is this confusion that infuriated the intellectuals but reassured the majority, who wished to be identifiable though not singled out. These houses were a protection, not only from the weather but also from a world in which human experience was harrowing and wounding.

135

'The worst of suburban life is that it wastes the one thing man cannot replace – life itself. To add hours of travel every week to a man's ordinary working day is just foolishly taking away all the advantages given by lessening hours in industry. I have been in houses at 7.30 or 8pm and heard the same tale: 'Not home yet. It takes him over an hour to get from work'. The kids don't see their father from week-end to week-end. He's merely the man who 'mucks about' in the garden every Sunday, to them. Young workers who ought to be learning their job as future citizens are arriving home too late and tired to do anything; they're making friends at their work, where there is no parental control over their choice, and are spending their leisure in the City.

'Don't forget that whenever a new suburb is built and folk leave a crowded area, they need over twice as many theatres, cinemas, churches, clubs, etc, as they did before. This is not an exaggeration, since – with 12 houses to the acre – all distances are increased, compared with, say, 60 to the acre. In point of fact most of the new suburbs have far less amenities than the crowded area. A suburb usually has no centre of its communal life. Meeting-places, churches, playing fields, are essentials of a suburb and should be there first, not several years after a suburb is built. Human life refuses to wait; and if a generation grows up before libraries, churches and public baths are provided, a generation is created which has learnt to do without them.

'The gardens are the best feature in a suburb. Most people like their own garden, but some would rather have public ones, with someone else to do the work in them.'

'Witness A' in a Radio Discussion on Suburbs or Satellites reported in *The Listener* (27 February 1935)

136

"IT'S A BARGAIN, LADY, AND A CHARMING PIECE. WHO KNOWS. IT MIGHT BE *THE* PERIOD FURNITURE NEXT YEAR THAT ALL MAYFAIR WAS WRENCHING THEIR 'AIR OUT TO GET HOLD OF."

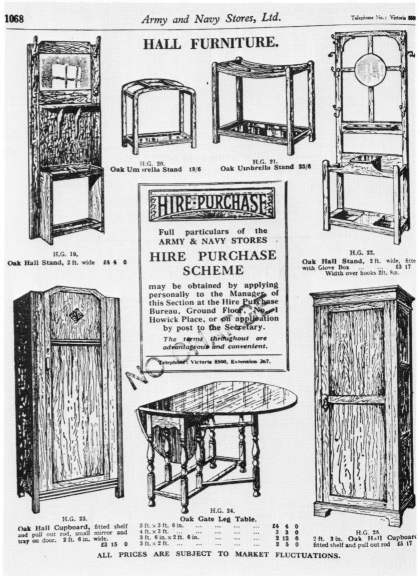

The suggestion that the majority of people wished to be identified by their homes was even more evident inside than out. Inside, indeed, there was often a positive wish to be singled out, and in 1935 the potential for diversity of style was immense. It was necessary only to walk through the front door of a lucky solvent owner's home to sense his predilections.

The humble occupier's opportunity for self-expression might be limited to the choice of a hall stand or table, but the very rich could state their case in a grand manner.

Of the entrance halls opposite that at the top left asserts an un-wavering sympathy with the modern movement. Bold and simple forms are relieved only by the foliage, arranged in a vase placed on table, both of which conform sympathetically to the containing curvilinear space in which they stand. Below this picture is another showing some cognisance of recent architecture developments, but acceptance of them is less sure. The window is in the fashionable 'Hollywood' style; the light bracket, table and vase all allude to other times and places.

More powerful allusions to the past are evident in the panelled hall, typical of the larger – perhaps detached – suburban house. Here confusion abounds between modern and traditional joinery details, modern door handles and 'olde worlde' lantern, carved settle and much favoured barometers, with Modernistic rug thrown in for good measure.

Crammed into the very narrow confines of the last hall, we see a determination to achieve Regency stripes and gilded grandeur – a grandeur, incidentally, which is in extreme contrast to the surrealist table of giant hand and glass top in another part of the same house.

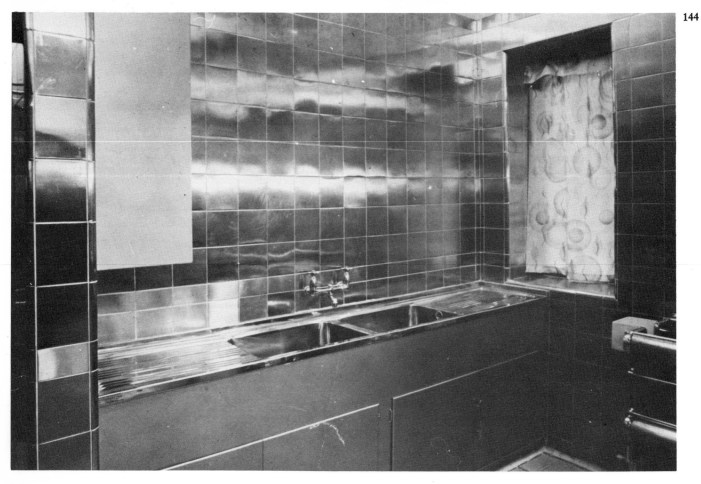

The move from entrance hall to kitchen in a lavishly appointed house of the middle 1930s could reveal a quite remarkable change of priorities.

Whereas other areas of the house were frequently witness to an occupier's romantic aspirations, often enough accompanied by a lack of design conviction, the kitchen demonstrated a more purposeful course.

Challenged to solve a number of practical and technical problems, conscious of the need to reduce unnecessary labour, aware of the availability of new materials and improved fuels, householders given the chance to decide about their kitchens abandoned an urge to idiosyncratic self-expression and fantasised, if they fantasised at all, about the establishment of a scientific attitude.

The two kitchens illustrated were in 1935 exhibitions. The views opposite show the Kemp House at the Ideal Home Exhibition. One of the lady visitors is pensive to see such wonders; the other may be giving the photographer the glad eye, but it would be more kindly to assume she is not only hugely delighted with what she sees but at the moment the shutter clicked she had realised how to make hubby indulge in some new equipment.

The picture above was taken in the British Art and Industry Exhibition. Not so dashing, perhaps, as the other, but the steel sink and work top with a refrigerator fitted below and extensive built-in cupboards and drawers in abundance are perhaps more practical – and certainly a far cry from the earlier scullery on page 38.

Moving with the food from kitchen to dining room the scientific attitude no longer holds sway.

The photographs on these pages are of dining room furniture available in 1935 from three London stores. On this page, chrome-plated steel tube structures and sycamore table top from Heals; opposite, the Deco Style in birds-eye maple or a spirited fusion of metal, timber and zebra skin from Fortnum & Mason; and in the top picture, Chippendale from Harrods.

147

148

149

'Wings' Brocade warp; woollen curtain by Elizabeth Peacock.
/*Bath Crafts Study Centre Collection*

In spite of the best efforts of the retail stores steel tube and zebra skin were not materials commonly found in the Dining Room of the 1930s. Chippendale there was certainly, and a good many other early styles.

Ruby M. Ayres' dining room was a space containing a nice accumulation of pieces, assembled it seems with confidence and affection. It is easy to imagine the pleasures of dining with Miss Ayres. The occasion might well be easy but sustaining, the conversation spirited yet controlled.

The picture below contains many of the same elements as the Ayres room and yet the feeling is quite different. Not, it could be argued, a happy room. Perhaps it is the juxtaposition of the modern ceiling light and the bulbous table legs, the uneasy relationship between the vases of flowers and the wallpaper, the two unrelated mirrors. The clock reminds guests of the time, the books are there in case the occasion is boring. ,Unfair! Unfair! cries the generous heart; but surely it was not a happy room.

The third dining room, above, boldly challenges comment. Tudoresque and Jacobethan elements could be combined with the real thing to achieve a massive, even ponderous, authority.

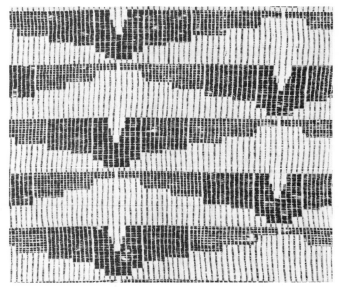

CURTAINS 1935

1936

3lb self raising flour   9½d
2lb granulated sugar   5d
1lb cocoa   1s 7d
1lb Indian tea   2s 8d
20 cigarettes   11½d
1 bottle whisky   12s 6d
1 pint pale ale   7d
3 tablets toilet soap   1s 6d
400 yard reel of cotton   4½d
1 yard scarlet flannel   3s
10lb wedding cake   £1 5s

Two enormous blocks of flats, both building in 1936, were both unlikely to have been considered a reasonable proposition even a few years earlier. Certainly they fly in the face of W. R. Davidge's comment on page 15 about the siting of block tenements.

The name of the development in the top picture, Dolphin Square, Westminster, suggests the scale of the project. We see only the unit on one side of the square which it contained. The scale of the development at Quarry Hill, Leeds, can be appreciated by the lower picture of the work in progress. It is also possible to appreciate that at Leeds the design embraces the rather stringent simplicity of the new architecture, whilst the London structure makes allusions, albeit emaciated and distorted allusions, to the great domestic architecture of Georgian London.

At Leeds the homes are intended by the local authority for the working classes; in London the homes are created by private enterprise for people who can afford the market price. It was a commonplace of the period that, with few and important exceptions, this distinction should exist. No moral points can be made; indeed, the unhappy truth is that whether housed in an ancient or modern enclosure, the rich were always more able and often more determined to maintain their property than the poor or the people who saw it as their duty to assist the poor.

Forty years after these pictures were taken, Dolphin Square had increased its value many times, the Quarry Hill Estate was in grave disarray. That is not the concern of this note. The importance in 1936 was that, in a nation of individuals dedicated to their own front door, such vast flat developments should have occurred at all.

'. . . . . *The dwelling place of the future is the Flat — so called because it usually is, and to distinguish it from the maisonette, which isn't. For this there are several reasons, mainly financial. What with rent, rates, stair-carpets, the depredations of mice, and the tendency of gardeners to bare their fangs if denied their lawful wage, a house of any kind costs a good deal to keep up. (That is especially true of those large country houses — colloquially known as "the stately homes of England" — where butlers are employed by half dozen and guests are provided with bicycles to enable them to reach the bath-room. But as the majority of these have now been converted into country clubs or dog-racing centres, they need not concern us at the moment.)*

'*The Servant Problem has also done its bit, and a bit more, towards depopularising houses. The most efficient housewife cannot run a large establishment without the help of minions; and nowadays minions — ay, and myrmidons to boot — are as scarce as second-hand coffins . . . . . .*

'*Hence the Flat. Reduced to its lowest terms (which, however, are seldom lower than £80 per annum), a flat is simply a portion of a house that has been converted but not entirely convinced. Since the primary purpose of flats is to enable at least five families to live where only one hung out before, thereby quintupling the landlord's income, they are apt to lack that spaciousness which characterises the Grand Central Terminal, New York. From the keen cat-swinger's point of view this is regrettable, but it enables the little woman to run the home single handed, with only the occasional help of a stout female in elastic-sided boots. And, anyway, dominoes is (or are) rapidly displacing cat-swinging as the favourite indoor pastime of the masses.*

'*In the last few years large blocks of flats — usually resembling Utopian prisons or Armenian glue factories — have sprung up all over the place, to the delight of some and the annoyance of many. These flats, though fitted with every up-to-date luxury — such as intermittent hot water and a porter with real brass buttons — are generally quite small, and getting smaller all the time, apparently. Thus the incoming tenant who has been accustomed to living in houses is liable at first to feel slightly crowded, as might a fly which, having been born and raised in the Albert Hall, was abruptly transferred in the evening of its days to a medium-sized dog-kennel.*'

from *How to Live in a Flat* by W. Heath Robinson and K. R. G. Browne (Hutchinson and Co Publishers Ltd 1936)

155

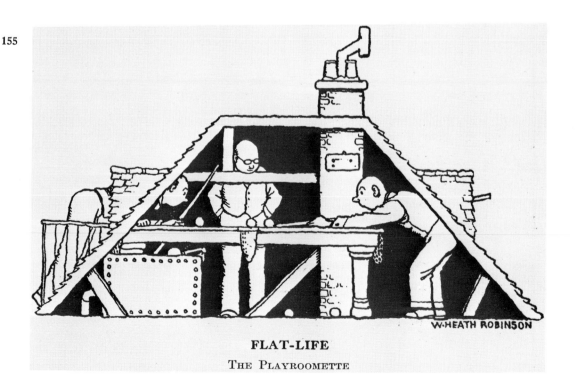

FLAT-LIFE

THE PLAYROOMETTE

To many English people of the inter-war years the Continental practice of living in flats came as something entirely new and for the majority it seemed unattractive. The cocktail was also new, and was much more happily received when it arrived from the USA.

Even the most insular Britisher knew by 1936 that cocktail more often meant a mixed drink with a spirit base than a horse with a docked tail. A new vogue was the cocktail cabinet and the cocktail party.

The cocktail cabinet proper was a cupboard, at a convenient height for pouring drinks, containing the ingredients, the receptacles and a variable number of manufacturing implements, of which the most important was the shaker. The mirror-faced cabinet designed by Alister Maynard is a classic of the genre.

For the more dedicated drinker the lounge could with propriety house a domestic bar. Here the whole performance of that high society hero, the barman with his own recipes, could be acted out for family and friends within the confines of home. A complete bar could be purchased from any reputable furnisher who was abreast the times.

There were, of course, some few who thought that playing bars was demonstrative beyond reason. For such reticent souls the room illustrated at left could well have been the answer: by day a library, but at cocktail time two built-in cupboards housing every Bacchanalian delight.

The picture above shows that all was not, in 1936, luxury unalloyed. The Ideal Home Exhibition demonstrates a storage unit made of biscuit tins and tea chests.

Silk, cotton and wool weave by Marianne Straub.
/*Bath Crafts Study Centre Collection*

The puzzle in these pictures of 1936 is: where are the cocktail cabinets?

Is that a cabinet just peeping into the right-hand side of the top picture opposite? Does it serve not only to complement the comfortable arrangement of bric-a-brac but also to lubricate the witching-hour?

What is the little unit with the reeded doors in the middle picture? It seems too shallow to house a vermouth bottle. So what is in the large cupboard of this collection of very new and very chic furnishings?

In the modern house, at the bottom, designed by Cameron Kirby and built at Bognor, the glasses are there. What's in the circular cupboard?

And finally, above, a room with surely everything of and for the times. But what are the two cupboards? Is the high one a writing bureau?

The answers are not given at the end of the book. Indeed, further questions may be added. Did anybody really buy a cocktail cabinet? Were cocktails really popular or only material for writers to describe? Did cocktail parties happen to anybody other than a few socialites? Statistics could well reveal more shadow than substance in the cult of the cocktail.

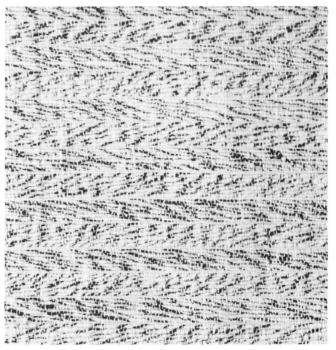

CURTAINS 1936

1937

This house, 66 Church Street London, was completed in 1937 to the designs of E. Maxwell Fry, a talented youg English architect, and Walter Gropius, a German pioneer of the modern movement in architecture, who, when political pressures forced him to leave his homeland, spent the first four years of his exile in England.

Like the house in the Jubilee Village of 1935 (page 90) there are curved elements built substantially of brick, which are stucco finished to give a bland up-to-date appearance. There the similarity ends. No 66 carries forward the story of the new architecture from Newways (page 42) Modern architecture was slow to gain acceptance in England, but by this time sufficient homes had been built for the Architectural Press to commission a substantial book, by F. R. S. Yorke, full of examples of *The Modern House in England*. There was, of course, some opposition. In particular many local authorities revealed an almost obsessive aesthetic prejudice. Bye-laws and technical regulations, which seemed to let through a deal of shoddy work on conventional structures, were frequently invoked to destroy an unusual idea. Nevertheless the new standards of design were slowly proving to be something more than a superficial decorative style. They were commending them selves to those people who could afford the thought necessary to a job in which form was not allowed to jeopardise content and in which intelligent, if occasionally unorthodox, planning was changing pretentious congestion into pleasurable space. This pleased the intellectuals without angering the majority who found it easier to ignore such radical stuff. It is only fair to note that whilst the building of No 66 pointed the way to a changed future in terms of aesthetic and structure, the accommodation provided smacked a little of the past – parents, three children, butler and two or three maid servants!

'In a working-class home – I am not thinking at the moment of the unemployed, but of comparatively prosperous homes – you breathe a warm, decent, deeply human atmosphere which it is not so easy to find elsewhere. I should say that a manual worker, if he is in steady work and drawing good wages – an 'if' which gets bigger and bigger – has a better chance of being happy than an 'educated' man. His home life seems to fall more naturally into a sane and comely shape. I have often been struck by the peculiar easy completeness, the perfect symmetry as it were, of a working-class interior at its best. Especially on winter evenings after tea, when the fire glows in the open range and dances mirrored in the steel fender, when Father, in shirt-sleeves, sits in the rocking chair at one side of the fire reading the racing finals, and Mother sits on the other with her sewing, and the children are happy with a pennorth of mint humbugs, and the dog lolls roasting himself on the rag mat – it is a good place to be in, provided that you can be not only in it but sufficiently of it to be taken for granted.

'This scene is still reduplicated in a majority of English homes, though not in so many as before the war. Its happiness depends mainly upon one question – whether Father is in work. But notice that the picture I have called up, of a working-class family sitting around the coal fire after kippers and strong tea, belongs only to our own moment of time and could not belong either to the future or the past. Skip forward two hundred years into the Utopian future, and the scene is totally different. Hardly one of the things I have imagined will still be there. In that age when there is no manual labour and everyone is 'educated', it is hardly likely that Father will still be a rough man with enlarged hands who likes to sit in shirt-sleeves and says "Ah wur coomin' oop street". And there won't be a coal fire in the grate, only some kind of invisible heater. The furniture will be made of rubber, glass, and steel. If there are still such things as evening papers there will certainly be no racing news in them, for gambling will be meaningless in a world where there is no poverty and the horse will have vanished from the face of the earth. Dogs, too, will have been suppressed on grounds of hygiene. And there won't be so many children, either, if the birth-controllers have their way. But move backwards into the Middle Ages and you are in a world equally foreign . . . .

'Curiously enough it is not the triumphs of modern engineering, nor the radio, nor the cinematograph, nor the five thousand novels which are published yearly, nor the crowds at Ascot and the Eton and Harrow match, but the memory of working-class interiors . . . . that reminds me that our age has not been altogether a bad one to live in.'

from *The Road to Wigan Pier* by George Orwell (Victor Gollancz 1937) by permission of Mrs. Sonia Brownell Orwell.

"Why 'The Rhododendrons'?"
"Well, they said the name was included in the price, and that was the longest one I knew."

Mrs Phillips, a very prosperous lady, purchased a house in Wimbledon and 'Frontenac' became a spectacular statement of the decorative fashions of the time. Externally the 'sunburst' device, common to articles as diverse as garden seats and radio cabinets, was well to the fore. Internally the richness of the mix can be deduced from the picture below of a part of the entrance hall.

At the other extreme of luxury living was architect Welles Coates' flat in Yeomans Row – an ample austerity created at the time when Coates was apt to remark that the only sensible place to sit was on the floor. Unlike the couple on page 31, he contrived to make the arrangement enjoyable. Between these extremes of abundance another, more generally accepted, statement of well-being is revealed in the Chivedon Place home of Oliver Hill, an eclectic architect who enjoyed considerable success in the 1930s. The main entertaining room, illustrated below right, contains within a quite severe form a juxtaposition of handsome materials and a wall decoration by Eric Gill. This suave reflection of an architecture thought by many to be ruthless and unsympathetic (if not downright politically dangerous) was of a manner accepted by an increasing number of the well-to-do.

168

If you feel, for a moment, that the combination of wealth, space and modernity in 1937 is an illusion of retrospection turn back to the two pictures of a room at No 5, Connaught Place. There's confidence for you. Even Picasso had arrived.

The occupiers of spacious and luxurious homes were a very small minority. For the majority a small garden was the only sizeable piece of space in which to expand. Even these people were fortunate as compared with the large numbers who lived in houses without garden.

Washing, as we see here at Morley, near Leeds, on occasion took precedence over traffic and for many the pavement outside the house was cared for with no less dedication than the interior. Doorstep and window sills would be cleaned with brown or white rubbing stone and the pavement itself scrubbed.

A game of cards by the front door was not an unusual sight and few children from street-homes could achieve adulthood without playing street-games. And in 1937 the Coronation of George VI meant a great many Royal parties: where better than in the street?

Oh! those parties!! A gift for every child from a benevolent Authority; the street transformed with flags, streamers and art of truly popular appeal; parents in jovial mood and acting as servants at a feast of every delight from tinned salmon sandwiches to tinned peaches!

Just occasionally living in a congested street was a privilege denied to the occupants of an ideal home.

CHEERS!

Always 'accept the invitation which will be given you to spend from Saturday to Monday in some country house', wrote Andre Maurois in the March issue of the magazine *Liliput*.

Maurois was doubtless referring to the Great Houses of England, where entertaining was still miraculously maintained in the pre-war style. The number of such houses was rapidly diminishing but as big houses disappeared small ones emerged.

In 1938 Newnes published *Saturday to Monday*, an anthology of entertainments for the week-end in the country. Its predecessor, *The Week End Book*, published in 1924 by the Nonesuch Press, was reissued by Penguin Books, having been reprinted 27 times in the interim. Harold Monro's introductory poem captures the mood; 'The train! The twelve o'clock for paradise . . . There you are waiting, little friendly house; those are your chimney stacks with you between. Surrounded by old trees and strolling cows . . .'.

As more and more families became car owners and as flats gained some acceptance as reasonable urban homes, the enthusiasm for country week-ends intensified. The 1938 Ideal Home Show featured Arundel Clarke's Week End Cottage and the countryside was splattered with evidence of the week-end home, even though many two-home owners felt a twinge of conscience when they thought of the homeless, and many second homes were as distasteful as Max Beerbohm found the static railway carriages of 1920.

If by unhappy chance one was neither the owner of a week-end cottage nor the likely guest of a Stately Home, there was still the hope of being invited to visit country houses as different from each other as Squadron Leader Lywood's home at Hartfield or Mr. Chermayeff's splendid new house at Halland. If the opportunity arose, few would resist M. Maurois' advice.

'We were bowling along in the old two-seater on our way to Totleigh Towers, self at the wheel, Jeeves at my side, the personal effects in the dickey. We had got off round about eleven-thirty, and the genial afternoon was now at its juiciest. It was one of those crisp, sunny, bracing days with a pleasant tang in the air . . . . . I had not failed to note that on a signpost which we had passed some little while back there had been inscribed the words "Totleigh-in-the-Wold, 8 miles." There now appeared before us through the trees a stately home of E.

'I braked the car.

' "Journey's End, Jeeves?"

' "So I should be disposed to imagine, sir."

'And so it proved. Having turned in at the gateway and fetched up at the front door, we were informed by the butler that this was indeed the lair of Sir Watkyn Bassett.

' . . . . . Old Bassett, I noted, had laid out his money to excellent advantage. I am a bit of a connoisseur of country houses, and I found this one well up to sample. Nice facade, spreading grounds, smoothly shaven lawns, and a general atmosphere of what is known as old world peace. Cows were mooing in the distance, sheep and birds respectively bleating and tootling, and from somewhere near at hand there came the report of a gun, indicating that someone was having a whirl at the local rabbits. Totleigh Towers might be a place where Man was vile, but undoubtedly every prospect pleased.

' . . . . . The cup of tea on arrival at a country house is a thing which, as a rule, I particularly enjoy. I like the crackling logs, the shaded lights, the scent of buttered toast, the general atmosphere of leisured cosiness. There is something that seems to speak to the deeps in me in the beaming smile of my hostess and the furtive whisper of my host, as he plucks at my elbow and says "Let's get out of here and go and have a whisky and soda in the gun-room." It is on such occasions as this, it has often been said, that you catch Bertram Wooster at his best.

' . . . . . Jeeves was right, I felt. The snail was on the wing and the lark on the thorn – or, rather, the other way round – and God was in His heaven and all right with the world.'

from *The Code of the Woosters* by P. G. Wodehouse (Herbert Jenkins Limited 1938) by permission of the Estate of P. G. Wodehouse and Baine & Jenkins Ltd.

179

"IT DOESN'T SEEM VERY HOMELIKE."
"WELL, MADAM, THIS IS REALLY A 'LUXURY FLAT.' "

Whether host or guest, the house-garden relationship would, weather permitting, be especially important to the pleasures of a country week end.

In Chermayeff's home at Halland the windows simply slid away to let the garden in. The arched terrace with its rattan chairs was a more normal 1930s location for tea or tiffin, whilst at the other extreme the new architecture made a roof terrace possible where the garden was inadequate.

The house at Southend shown on the right, designed by Welles Coates, suggests the delights of this new freedom.

The picture above demonstrates the considerable refinement of a terrace related to entertaining rooms with an outside staircase to the bedrooms. A nice provision for an elegant retreat after the nightcap.

The retreat after the nightcap could be to a bedroom in one of many moods and here are two lively extremes. It is unlikely that many people could enjoy both – even for a weekend. A good number would be incapable of enjoying either.

The bed on this page and the mirror fronted chest of drawers were available from Fortnum & Mason. Many similar but lesser dream-boats were no doubt available from lesser stores throughout the land.

The room opposite, and its dressing table, was a deter-minedly up to the minute one-off designed with scrupulous care for the house at Halland.

Both pictures illustrate aspects of 1930s wealth which, with hindsight, it would be possible to criticise either for social irresponsibility or self-indulgence. One could be ridiculed for fantasising absurdly in a time of crisis, the other for pushing a concern with modernity to an absurd degree. In the face of such zestful enthusiasm hindsight of this sort would be both ungenerous and unnatural.

Screen printed glazed cotton designed by Ashley Havinden.
/*Crown Copyright, Victoria and Albert Museum*

1938 bedrooms did not generally exhibit aesthetic extremes. Nevertheless there was diversity in abundance. Denise Robins' bedroom at Furnace Pond Cottage in Sussex eschews somnolent grandeur, but achieves a pretty cosiness with many a reference to past styles. On the other hand, for those who had rejected evocation but could not face modernism, Gordon Russell continued his great work. In 1938 he produced simple oak bedroom furniture 'paricularly suitable for a cottage', which happily extended the best traditions of English furniture-making in harmony with modern thought.

With all this to choose from the majority of 1938 bedrooms had characteristics in common with that illustrated above.

CURTAINS 1938

1939

3lb self raising flour	9½d
2lb granulated sugar	5d
1lb cocoa	1s 9d
1lb Indian tea	3s
20 cigarettes	11½d
1 bottle whisky	12s 6d
1 pint pale ale	7d
3 tablets toilet soap	1s 6d
400 yard reel of cotton	5d
1 yard scarlet flannel	3s 3d
10lb wedding cake	£1 5s

On 1 May 1939 there was a celebration of the four millionth house to be built in Britain since the end of the World War in 1918.

Just as the problem seemed to be changing from the desparate task of providing enough homes to the more pleasant task of improving the quality of the least satisfactory, the building industry's resources were diverted to other matters.

On 3 September at 11.15am Prime Minister Neville Chamberlain announced on the wireless that 'a situation in which no word given by Germany's ruler could be trusted and no people or country could feel themselves safe, had become intolerable.' Britain was at war again. It was not a complete surprise. Trench digging had been going on for some time. Most people had tried on their gas masks and some spoke of a sense of relief that a comprehensible situation had replaced a war of nerves.

Street lighting was extinguished. Mothers scoured the shops for material to black out windows. Fathers pasted paper strips or net on the panes to prevent flying glass; some four million children wondered what it would be like to be evacuated to homes in the country or Canada or the USA. It was a time of major change.

In the event about one and a half million children moved to somebody else's place-in-the-country. Many young people left home to join the armed forces.

For the people left behind emotional disturbance was linked with physical change. Air raid shelters were the new home extension. The top picture shows deliveries of metal units for sinking into the garden, below are brick built shelters in Peckham Street. Many owners improvised protection in their house. Though the importance of a shelter to survival was understood, the shelter was not readily accepted as an ideal home from home.

'Sitting by a blazing fire on an October evening, in a room lit by lamps and candles, I could not yesterday help counting my treasures and wondering how many of them may never be enjoyed by such as I again. To have walked across the misty fields of autumn and come out of the raw afternoon with tingling veins and a memory of sad elms and crimson and gold gleaming down the sentenced hedges, to feel the embracing warmth of the house even before one reaches the line of its latticed, lighted windows, to raise the latch and enter into one's own home – not a concrete and steel box in a skyscraper, but a solid, ancient house that has seen successive generations of children bred and won the love of its owners for centuries – is to.enjoy great wealth. It is a wealth of a kind which was common enough a generation or two back, but which today is becoming increasingly rare. Probably not one in ten of our new urban population, town dwellers now for at least four generations, would recognise it. Its continuance is threatened by every kind of modern development . . . . I doubt whether our children's children will see its like.

'I suppose that when this war is over, we shall celebrate its passing in some appropriate fashion. At that moment we shall recall its beginning. Not bugles, but sirens, will probably sound the coming of Armistice and the return to the ways, however changed, of peace. Nor, I imagine, will the hour for the "cease fire" be fixed, as on the last occasion, at eleven in the morning. Rather our imaginative rulers – certainly if Mr. Churchill is still among them – will choose eleven at night. For some hours before the moment of release and final victory, we shall grope about in our accustomed darkness. Even torches will not be used that night, and in London the funeral taxis will crawl through the streets without even the formality of sidelights. Then, on the last stroke of eleven, in a single blinding flash, our darkness will be lightened. Amid the wailing of air-raid sirens, the blowing of whistles and the sounding of rattles, every light in London will be turned on at once. Piccadilly will be its old self, blazing with vulgar, coloured revolving advertisements and Eros restored will be floodlit. Cars will dash through the streets with their headlights on and from the parks will ascend, not pale, discreet blimps but fireworks. On every height in the shires the beacons will burst into flame. It will be a national carnaval of light and every window will be uncurtained to the watching night; at that moment it will seem as though nothing on the whole of God's universe is dimmed.'

Arthur Bryant writing in *Illustrated London News* (30 October 1937 and 9 December 1939)

191

"My dear, it's as safe as houses."

192

195

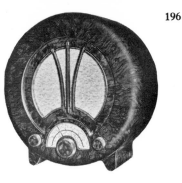

196

1939 will go down in history as Television Year, announced the manufacturers Ekco in a brochure to their retailers, encouraging them to take advantage of lower prices, better programmes and longer transmission hours. The time certainly seemed right for a big selling campaign to the householders of the land. Ekco's add-on vision unit TA201, which connected to a radio set, cost £23 2s and a console model scheduled for release later in the year, was to cost £31 10s.

Alas! History was to remember 1939 for other things. The BBC had started the first regular high-definition television service in November 1936; in February 1938 the Postmaster General announced that, after a deal of experiment, transmission standards would remain substantially unaltered for at least three years; in April 1938 Sunday programmes were introduced. But in September 1939 the transmission service was closed down and the twenty thousand or so owners of a receiver suddenly found themselves with a useless piece of equipment.

Nine million radio licence holders continued to be served and Ekco could boast receivers costing as little as £6 6s for battery-powered model B39 to as much as £52 10s for their latest press-button, motor-controlled autoradiogram.

For table models the horizontal form was coming in, but those illustrated here were still characteristic of the time (moulded plastic cabinets in 'figured walnut finish' for the conservative or black and chrome for the moderns). Purpose-built console models for the wealthy enthusiast showed even more remarked respect for individual taste.

1939 was not television year, but Radio moved into a position of importance in home life unequalled before or since.

193

194

197

198

The development of cheap paperback editions during the 1930s meant the reading and owning of books was possible to a wider public than ever before and by 1939 few English homes were without any books at all. Generally speaking they were well cared for, as witness the remarkable 1939 telephone directory stand.

The sort of books and the way they were accommodated varied enormously from, at one extreme, a library of leather-bound volumes like the one in Goodhart Rendel's own home, to a few paperbacks in a booknest. More normally some corner of a living room would have a few well-stocked shelves, like those in the bottom picture.

As with listening-in, the advent of war increased rather than diminished the habit of reading and the paperback offered other advantages beside the economic one. They were just right for stuffing into a kit-bag or taking down to the air-raid shelter.

New Curtains, suddenly needed by virtually every home in England, could be any material, style or design so long as no light shone through.

No telly, gas masks ranged with tea and sugar on the kitchen shelves, the children away in some remote country district and the lads in uniform, heaven knows where and having to look after themselves.

For the young the events of the winter of 1939 offered some sense of adventure to come; for those who had been setting up home at the end of the last war there were unhappy memories and an uneasy concern for the family which had grown in the interim; and for the very elderly there was often terror of new unknowns.

The government did its best to reassure. The cut-away street shelter in the picture opposite showed how cosy and friendly the forbidding brick boxes in the street could be made. Take your wireless, a book, a blanket; arrange to make a cup of tea; and all will be well.

People smiled and determined to make the best of things. Let's buy ten pounds of sugar to see us through to peacetime, whispered the provident; have a pint and hope for the best, said the philosophers; let's knit harder for the lads in the forces, said the philanthropists. But the smile of a father helping his family into their home extension in the garden was, we may presume, unusually forced.

For a little while the peace of home was at an end.

1939 THE END

The authors and publishers wish to thank all those people and organisations mentioned in the text or listed below for reproduction permissions whether of text or pictures. The numbers below relate to those identifying illustrations.

1 The London Transport Executive
2 Fox Photos
3 The Bournville Village Trust
4 *The Architectural Review*
5–6 Radio Times Hulton Picture Library
7 Ward Associates, London
8 *Punch*
9 Associated Newspapers Group
10 The Science Museum, London
11–12 Associated Newspapers Group
13 Harrods, London
14 The Bournville Village Trust
15 Aerofilms Limited
16 The Greater London Council
17 *Punch*
18–20 The Bournville Village Trust
21 The Greater London Council
22 *Punch*
23 Associated Newspapers Group
24 The Mansell Collection
25 Heal and Son, London
26 The Mansell Collection
27–28 Radio Times Hulton Picture Library
29 The Bournville Village Trust
30–31 Duckworth and Company Limited
32 *Punch*
33 The Mansell Collection
34–35 Gordon Russell Limited, Broadway
36–38 Duckworth and Company Limited
39–40 Aerofilms Limited
41 The London Transport Executive
42 *Punch*
43 A+N, London
44–48 The Bournville Village Trust
49 The Mansell Collection
50 Radio Times Hulton Picture Library
51 The Bournville Village Trust
52 *Punch*
53 Associated Newspapers Group
54 A + N, London
55 Radio Times Hulton Picture Library
56 *The Architects Journal*
57 The Greater London Council
58 Radio Times Hulton Picture Library
59 *The Architectural Review*
60 *Punch*
61–64 *The Architectural Review*
65 Radio Times Hulton Picture Library
66 *Punch*
67 The Science Museum, London
68 John Crossley and Sons Limited, Halifax
69 Gordon Russell Limited, Broadway
70 Aerofilms Limited
71 *Punch*
72 The Mansell Collection
73 Dryad
74 Radio Times Hulton Picture Library
75–76 Millar & Harris, London
77 Victoria & Albert Museum, London
78 Radio Times Hulton Picture Library
79 Aerofilms Limited
80 *Punch*
81–83 Associated Newspapers Group
84–85 Millar & Harris, London
86 Gordon Russell Limited, Broadway
87 Aerofilms Limited
88 *The Architects Journal*
89 *Daily Express* Publications
90 The Walker Art Gallery, Liverpool
91 Ward Associates, London

92 A + N, London
93 Heal and Son, London
94 Radio Times Hulton Picture Library
95 Heal and Son, London
96–98 Victoria & Albert Museum, London
99–100 Aerofilms Limited
101 *Punch*
102–106 Fox Photos
107 *Punch*
108–109 Pye Limited, Cambridge
110–111 National Film Archive
112 Radio Times Hulton Picture Library
113–114 Associated Newspapers Group
115 The Bournville Village Trust
116–117 Radio Times Hulton Picture Library
118 *Punch*
119–124 Heal and Son, London
125–126 Millar & Harris, London
127 *The Architectural Review*
128 The Bournville Village Trust
129–130 *The Architects Journal*
131 *Punch*
132 *The Architects Journal*
133 The Bournville Village Trust
134 Associated Newspapers Group
135 Ward Associates, London
136 *Punch*
137 Millar & Harris, London
138 A + N, London
139 Millar & Harris, London
140 Fox Photos
141–142 Millar & Harris, London
143–144 Associated Newspapers Group
145 *The Architectural Review*
146 Heal and Son, London
147–149 Millar & Harris, London

150 Radio Times Hulton Picture Library
151–152 Fox Photos
153 *The Architects Journal*
154 Areofilms Limited
155 Hutchinson Publishing Group Limited
156–158 Millar & Harris, London
159 Associated Newspapers Group
160 Radio Times Hulton Picture Library
161 Millar & Harris, London
162 *The Architectural Review*
163 Fox Photos
164 *The Architectural Review*
165 Ward Associates, London
166 *Punch*
167–172 Millar & Harris, London
173 Fox Photos
174 The Mansell Collection
175–176 Fox Photos
177 Millar & Harris, London
178 *The Architectural Review*
179 *Punch*
180 *The Architectural Review*
181–184 Millar & Harris, London
185 *The Architectural Review*
186 Radio Times Hulton Picture Library
187 Gordon Russell Limited, Broadway
188 Fox Photos
189–190 Radio Times Hulton Picture Library
191 *Punch*
192–194 Millar & Harris, London
195–198 Pye Limited, Cambridge
199–200 Millar & Harris, London
201–203 *The Architectural Review*
204–205 Fox Photos
206–207 Radio Times Hulton Picture Library
208 The London Transport Executive

208